Living before an era of 'Christendom', Irenaeus of Lyons, the first great theologian of the Church, has much to offer us today. This volume is an excellent introduction to his life and works, covering all aspects of his theology, including, notably, the pastoral and the political. It is highly recommended.

John Behr
Regius Chair in Humanities,
University of Aberdeen, Aberdeen

Inviting, insightful, and inspiring. This is now the best place to begin your introduction to the life and life-changing impact of Irenaeus of Lyons. We are all in Presley's debt.

D. Jeffrey Bingham
Research Professor of Historical Theology,
Southwestern Seminary, Fort Worth, Texas

EARLY CHURCH FATHERS
SERIES EDITORS: MICHAEL A. G. HAYKIN
& SHAWN J. WILHITE

IRENAEUS
OF LYONS

HIS LIFE & IMPACT

STEPHEN O. PRESLEY

CHRISTIAN
FOCUS

Copyright © Stephen O. Presley 2025

paperback ISBN 978-1-5271-1301-5
ebook ISBN 978-1-5271-1390-9

10 9 8 7 6 5 4 3 2 1

Published in 2025
by
Christian Focus Publications Ltd,
Geanies House, Fearn, Ross-shire,
IV20 1TW, Great Britain.

www.christianfocus.com

Cover design by MOOSE77

Printed and bound by
Bell & Bain, Glasgow

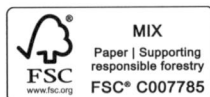

FSC
www.fsc.org

MIX
Paper | Supporting
responsible forestry
FSC® C007785

CONTENTS

Series Preface 9

Introduction..13

1. Engaging Culture...25

2. A Theological System 49

3. Pastoral Ministry..67

4. The Spiritual Life..93

5. Christian Citizenship 111

6. Cultural Apologetics..129

Conclusion..143

DEDICATION

To my mentor and friend

D. J. B.

whose love for the Christian tradition inspired many.

On Reading the Church Fathers

By common definition, the Church Fathers are those early Christian authors who wrote between the close of the first century, right after the death of the last of the apostles, namely the apostle John, and the middle of the eighth century. In other words, those figures who were active in the life of the church between Ignatius of Antioch and Clement of Rome, who penned writings at the very beginning of the second century, and the Venerable Bede and John of Damascus, who stood at the close of antiquity and the onset of the Middle Ages. Far too many Evangelicals in the modern day know next to nothing about these figures. I will never forget being asked to give a mini-history conference at a church in southern Ontario. I suggested three talks on three figures from Latin-speaking North Africa: Perpetua, Cyprian, and Augustine. The leadership of the church came back to me seeking a different set of names, since they had never heard of the first two figures, and while they had heard of the third name, the famous bishop of Hippo Regius, they really knew nothing about him. I gave them another list of post-Reformation figures for the mini-conference, but privately thought that not knowing anything about these figures was possibly a very good reason to have a conference on them! I suspect that such ignorance is quite widespread among those who call themselves Evangelicals—hence the importance of this small series of studies on a select number of Church Fathers, to educate and inform God's people about their forebears in the faith.

Past Appreciation for the Fathers

How different is the modern situation from the past, when many of our Evangelical and Reformed forebears knew and treasured the writings of the ancient church. The French Reformer John Calvin, for example, was ever a keen student of the Church Fathers. He did not always agree with them, even when it came to one of his favorite authors, namely Augustine. But he was deeply aware of the value of knowing their thoughts and drawing upon the riches of their written works for elucidating the Christian faith in his own day. And in the seventeenth century, the Puritan theologian John Owen, rightly called the "Calvin of England" by some of his contemporaries, was not slow to turn to the experience of the one he called "holy Austin," namely Augustine, to provide him with a pattern of God the Holy Spirit's work in conversion.

Yet again, when the Particular Baptist John Gill was faced with the anti-Trinitarianism of the Deist movement in the early eighteenth century, and other Protestant bodies—for instance, the English Presbyterians, the General Baptists, and large tracts of Anglicanism—were unable to retain a firm grasp on this utterly vital biblical doctrine, Gill turned to the Fathers to help him elucidate the biblical teaching regarding the blessed Trinity. Gill's example in this regard influenced other Baptists such as John Sutcliff, pastor of the Baptist cause in Olney, where John Newton also ministered. Sutcliff was so impressed by the *Letter* to *Diognetus*, which he wrongly supposed to have been written by Justin Martyr, that he translated it for *The Biblical Magazine*, a Calvinistic publication with a small circulation. He sent it to the editor of this periodical with the commendation that this second-century work is "one of the most valuable pieces of ecclesiastical antiquity."

One Final Caveat

One final word about the Fathers recommended in this small series of essays. The Fathers are not Scripture; they are senior conversation partners about Scripture and its meaning. We listen to them respectfully but are not afraid to disagree when they err. As the Reformers rightly argued, the writings of the Fathers must be subject to Scripture. John Jewel, the Anglican apologist, put it well when he stated in 1562:

> But what say we of the fathers, Augustine, Ambrose, Jerome, Cyprian, etc.? What shall we think of them, or what account may we make of them? They be interpreters of the word of God. They were learned men, and learned fathers; the instruments of the mercy of God, and vessels full of grace. We despise them not, we read them, we reverence them, and give thanks unto God for them. They were witnesses unto the truth, they were worthy pillars and ornaments in the church of God. Yet may they not be compared with the word of God. We may not build upon them: we may not make them the foundation and warrant of our conscience: we may not put our trust in them. Our trust is in the name of the Lord.

Michael A. G. Haykin
The Southern Baptist Theological Seminary
Louisville, Kentucky, U.S.A

Shawn J. Wilhite
California Baptist University
Riverside, California.

INTRODUCTION

My family and I stood before the chain-linked fence gazing at the remains of an old Roman amphitheater in Lyons, France. I held in my hand a book containing an ancient letter describing the Christian martyrs who died on these grounds in A.D. 177. The letter, likely written by a presbyter named Irenaeus, depicts a series of brutal persecutions that ravaged the ancient Christian community in Lyons and the neighboring city of Vienne. This letter was addressed to a certain Eleutherus, the bishop in Rome (c. A.D. 178–189), and mentioned that the church leadership in Lyons "requested our brother and companion Irenaeus to carry this epistle to you." Irenaeus was highly esteemed in the church of Lyons. The letter calls him a "presbyter of the church" and requests that Eleutherus consider Irenaeus "as one who is zealous for the covenant of Christ."[1]

Excepting these occasions of persecution, the second century was a relatively stable time, known as the Antonine era, when

---

1.　Translations of this letter are from: Eusebius of Caesarea, *The History of the Church: A New Translation*, translated by Jeremy M. Schott (Oakland: University of California Press, 2019).

the Roman Empire was at its height. Thanks to Roman rule, Irenaeus remarks that the world is at peace, and "we can travel and sail without fear."[2] But the church was also growing slowly. Through the missionary efforts begun by Paul and the other apostles, Christian leaders were evangelizing throughout the ancient world. The church was embedded within the fabric of the empire. Even though they lived as citizens of Rome, they followed a different pattern of life that destabilized the religious and philosophical ethos that bound the Roman world together. By the late second century the Romans and the Gallic tribes in the region of Lyons had had enough. They conspired together and turned their fury upon the Christians.

As my family and I stared at the crumbling remains of the stadium seating encircling the arena, it was easy to imagine the crowd gathered, cheering for the death of the Christians. I slowly began to read aloud the account of the persecution. The ominous opening lines capture the extreme cruelty of the persecution: "Now, then, the magnitude of the oppression in this place, the extent of the Gentiles' rage against the saints, and what the blessed martyrs endured, we are not capable of describing accurately in speech nor can they be comprehended in writing."[3] And they did suffer. "For the adversary attacked with all [his] might," the letter continues, "offering already a kind of preview of when he will come with impunity."[4] These ancient Christians were barred from civic life. Not only were they "shut out of buildings, baths, and agoras," the text reads, but the Christians report that "we were universally banned from appearing in any place whatsoever."[5]

---

2. *Haer* 4.30.3. Translations are taken from: Irenaeus, *Against the Heresies: Books 4 and 5*, translated by Dominic J. Unger and Scott D. Moringiello, Ancient Christian Writers 72 (New York: Newman Press, 2024).

3. Eusebius, *Ecclesiastical History*, 5.1.4.

4. Eusebius, *History of the Church*, 5.1.5.

5. Eusebius, *History of the Church*, 5.1.5.

Gazing at the large circular dirt-covered pad where these martyrdoms took place, we listened to the stories of suffering. Christians with names like Vettius Epagathus, Maturus, Sanctus, Blandina, Attalus, Alexander, and Pothinus. Each made bold confessions of Christ before the jeering crowd. Pothinus, the elderly bishop of the church in Lyons, was already over ninety years old and must have been one of the earliest members of the community. The letter culminates in the martyrdom of Blandina, a woman who was the last one alive. When she was accused, she responded confidently, "I am a Christian, and there is no evil done amongst us," a response that encouraged others who were there. They showed her no mercy; she was tortured and ravished to the point that even the Roman authorities said there was nothing left to do to her.

Not all the Christians were faithful unto death. Some ten succumbed to the pressure and worshiped the pagan gods so they could go free. But many remained committed to Christ and reported that they felt that the grace of God "marshaled together the weak, and braced them with firm supports capable by their endurance of absorbing all the rage of the enemy that was directed against them."[6] Today, a stone pillar stands in the middle of the worn-down pad signifying those who had given their lives for the cause of Christ on that very spot.

When I finished the letter, we all stood gazing down upon the soil, wondering how the Christian community managed to pick up the pieces and carry on. Irenaeus took over the leadership of the church in Lyons after these events, and this biography explores his vision for ministry which led him and others through these tumultuous times. For those who are unfamiliar with Irenaeus' writings, I hope this biography serves as a good introduction to one of the most fascinating theologians in the early church. For those more familiar with his work, I try to synthesize his contribution from a few perspectives that are not

---

6.   Eusebius, *History of the Church*, 5.1.5.

often discussed, such as his theological method, his vision of the spiritual life, his view of citizenship, and his perspective on pastoral ministry. I hope these approaches provide some fresh perspectives on Irenaeus' important contributions.

Biography

But before I move on to explain these features of Irenaeus' thought, I want to begin with a few points of background. We have very limited details about Irenaeus' life, but there are enough data points to make some general observations. Irenaeus was born between A.D. 130-140 in the town of Smyrna, located in Asia minor.[7] Not much is known about his early years, but at some point, he encountered the preaching of Polycarp (d. A.D. 155-56). Polycarp was a well-known Christian leader in Asia Minor, who reportedly had conversations with the apostle John. He wrote at least one letter that is extant, Polycarp's letter to the Philippians, and his final moments were recorded in an ancient account known as the *Martyrdom of Polycarp*.

In a letter to a friend named Florinus, Irenaeus describes the impact his interactions with Polycarp had upon him.[8] The occasion for the letter is Florinus' growing interest in the various Gnostic sects that have been infiltrating the church. Irenaeus recalls hearing Polycarp and other presbyters describing their conversations with certain apostles and others who were familiar with the apostolic community. "For I knew you [Florinus] when I was still a boy in lower Asia, with Polycarp," Irenaeus writes, "when you were doing splendidly in the kingly hall, and trying to garner his respect."[9] This appears to be a kind of discipleship setting, where Polycarp is instructing a group on the apostolic teaching. Irenaeus provides a detailed account, saying, "I remember the events of that time better than what

---

7.   Eric Osborn, *Irenaeus of Lyons* (Cambridge: Cambridge University Press, 2001), 2.

8.   The *Letter to Florinus* is recorded in Eusebius, *History of the Church*, 5.20.4-8.

9.   Eusebius, *History of the Church*, 5.20.5. See also *Haer.* 3.3.4.

has happened recently."[10] He describes the way he was moved by Polycarp's words and the persuasiveness of his character of his life and ministry. He also recounts the conversations Polycarp had with the apostle John and others who were eyewitnesses of the Lord's ministry. Speaking of Polycarp, Irenaeus writes, "I listened to it all diligently, recording it not on papyrus, but in my heart. And by the grace of God, I always ruminate on them truly."[11] From these descriptions, it seems that Irenaeus spent a rather significant amount of time with Polycarp, absorbing his instruction.[12]

At some point, Irenaeus made his way west to Rome and then up to Lyons to join the community on the outskirts of the Roman Empire. We do not know the path he took to get there. He was probably interacting with Christian leaders in Asia Minor and it is possible that he accompanied Polycarp on some of his visits to Rome, such as the time Polycarp visited Rome two years before his martyrdom to discuss the dating of Easter.[13] Whatever the case, by the latter half of the second century, Irenaeus finds himself working with the church in Lyons. He describes his community as those who "live among the Celts."[14] Lyons was the principle city of the region and fertile ground for planting and building a Christian community. The martyrs of Lyons, mention above, seem to include founders of the church, so the church must have been planted in the early to mid-second

10. Eusebius, *History of the Church*, 5.20.6.

11. Eusebius, *History of the Church*, 5.20.7.

12. John Behr, *Irenaeus of Lyons: Identifying Christianity* (Oxford: Oxford University Press, 2013), 63.

13. *Haer* 3.3.4. Eusebius, *History of the Church*, 5.24.12–17. All translations of Irenaeus, *Against Heresies* 3 are taken from: Irenaeus, *Against the Heresies: Book 3*, translated by Dominic J. Unger and Irenaeus M. C. Steenberg, Ancient Christian Writers 64 (New York: Newman Press, 2012).

14. *Haer* 1.pf.3.

century.[15] We know little about Irenaeus' death, but there is no doubt about the impact he has had on the church.

Writings

Irenaeus was clearly educated, theologically astute, and deeply immersed in Scripture. Besides Polycarp, he mentions interactions with a variety of Christian leaders and texts including Papias, Justin Martyr, *1 Clement*, Ignatius of Antioch, *Shepherd of Hermas*, and other elders of the church. I assume that he learned a great deal from these and other Christian theologians of the era. We also know, as I mentioned above, that Irenaeus had interactions with Eleutherus, the bishop in Rome and Victor who followed him in that position.

His writings shows a broad awareness of the religious and philosophical communities in the ancient world. He is familiar with the philosophical traditions, especially the writings of Middle Platonism. He mentions such philosophers as Plato, Aristotle, the Stoics, Homer, Democritas, and Hereclitus.[16] The opening book of *Against Heresies* records a Homeric cento that was a common literary exercise in a Grammaticus, an ancient grammar school.[17] He demonstrates interactions with various Gnostic groups that were practicing their faith in this region around the Rhone.[18]

But he is humble about his education too. He claims that he is not "accustomed to writing books, or practiced in the art of rhetoric."[19] Living among the Celts, he must "transact practically everything in a barbarous tongue," so the reader should not expect to find the "rhetorical art, which we have

---

15. Behr, *Identifying Christianity*, 19.

16. See *Haer* 2.14.1–9.

17. *Haer* 1.9.4. All translations of *Against Heresies* 1 are taken from: Irenaeus, *Against the Heresies, Book 1*, translated by Dominic J. Unger and John J. Dillion, Ancient Christian Writers 55 (New York: Newman Press, 1992).

18. *Haer* 1.13.7.

19. *Haer* 1.pf.2.

never learned, or the craft of writing, in which we have not had practice, or elegant style and persuasiveness, with which we are not familiar."[20] But this self-deprecation, too, may be part of his rhetorical moves.

The early Church historian Eusebius gives a summary of Irenaeus' writings in his possession that suggest he has more literary skills than he is letting on. Most of these writings are no longer available to us, but they show Irenaeus' extensive literary output. Eusebius mentions a work titled, *On Knowledge*, which was written against the Hellenes, a work Eusebius describes as "a book of various discussions, in which he mentions the Letter to the Hebrews and the so-called Wisdom of Solomon, setting down certain passages from them."[21] He also wrote two letters to Florinus, one entitled *On Monarchy or the Fact That God Is Not the Maker of Evils*, and another entitled *On the Ogdoad*, which he wrote when Florinus was turning to Valentinianism.[22] Eusebius also mentions another letter written to Victor, one that was about Florinus, and a text called *On Schism* about Blastus.[23] Finally, the letter mentioned at the opening of this chapter, *Letter of the Churches of Vienne and Lyons to the Churches of Asia and Phrygia*, was likely penned by Irenaeus.[24]

Only two of Irenaeus' works survive, but they demonstrate two key concerns of his ministry: discipleship and apologetics. The first work, entitled *The Demonstration of the Apostolic Preaching*, is shorter, only one hundred paragraphs.[25] The word "demonstration" (Greek, *epideixis*) is a common rhetorical term meaning a proof or exhibition. In this case Ireaneus offers a demonstration or proof of the apostolic preaching. The work is

---

20. *Haer* 1.pf.3.

21. Eusebius, *History of the Church*, 5.26.

22. Eusebius, *History of the Church*, 5.20.1.

23. Eusebius, *History of the Church*, 5.20.1.

24. Eusebius, *History of the Church*, 5.1–3.

25. Eusebius, *History of the Church*, 5.26.

written to a friend named Marcianus, who was likely a Christian leader involved in the training of new converts, or a process known as *catechesis* (Greek for "teaching" or "instruction"). Even a cursory reading of the *Demonstration* reveals a substantial depth of biblical knowledge. Irenaeus traces the storyline of Scripture, discusses the unity of the covenants in Christ, and explains how Christ fulfills many passages from the prophets. He also discusses the church, with allusions to the story of Acts, and frames the work with references to the heretical teaching that is circulating. All of these literary features help demonstrate Irenaeus' perspective on the content and purpose of catechetical instruction.

Irenaeus is most widely known for his longer and more substantial work entitled *The Refutation and Overthrowal of Knowledge Falsely So-Called*, though it is often referred to by its shorter title, *Against Heresies*.[26] This work is a massive five-volume refutation of the various streams of Gnosticism and other heretical leaders and communities that were vying for cultural influence in the ancient world. The first book catalogs the different heretical leaders and groups. It reads like a set of Wikipedia entries for the different streams of Gnosticism and includes a discussion of their origins, key leaders, and worldview, along with Irenaeus' own personal commentary on the ways they deviate from the Scriptures. The second book examines some key points of doctrine in their systems and explains the ways they differ from the church's theological vision. The last three books offer reflections upon different theological issues that help explain the error of the Gnostics. In the past, many scholars have criticized the structure and coherence of this work; Irenaeus' writing is profoundly complex in places. But more

---

26. *Haer* 4.pf.1; Eusebius, *History of the Church*, 5.7.1. Originally written in Greek, these texts mostly survive in translations including Latin, Armenian, Syric, and some Greek fragments.

recent scholarship has found unity within the complexity.[27] To understand Irenaeus' writings, a reader needs to sit with them for a while, mulling over his theological perspective.

Irenaeus' background and literary output reveals an active ministry life, forged amid an entrenched Roman culture. Irenaeus learned to navigate this world with faith and fortitude, and I believe his example can help guide us to do the same.

Summary of Chapters

This is an intellectual biography of Irenaeus, tracing some of the key themes that animate his ministry and spiritual life. In chapter one, I delve into Irenaeus' setting, explaining his perceptions of Jews, Greco-Roman philosophers, and Gnostics. Situated among these groups, Irenaeus' most intense criticisms were levied against the Gnostics; they present the pressing ministry challenges before him. The health of his community demanded a careful apologetic response to these groups percolating through the ancient world and so, in different ways, these groups help Irenaeus articulate how to live the Christian life.

In chapter two, I start with first principles, explaining Irenaeus' perception of reality. God is the source of all truth, so only those who believe in God can comprehend truth. I also explain the general contours of Irenaeus' theological system, which he terms the rule of faith. The rule emerges from Scripture and offers a faithful summary of what Scripture teaches. Then I discuss Irenaeus' theological method, the interaction between faith and reason that guides his pastoral and apologetic efforts.

In chapter three, I discuss his vision of pastoral ministry. There are two essential ingredients to the pastoral life: sound teaching and a blameless life. The pastor should be an exemplar in wisdom and virtue, living an upright and holy life, and expounding the Scriptures in all faithfulness. Other essential

---

27. Mary Ann Donovan, *One Right Reading?* (Collegeville, MN: The Liturgical Press, 1997), 7.

features of pastoral work include baptism, Eucharist, prayer, and martyrdom. Each of these prepare the faithful for the holy life, both in the present age and the age to come. He sees the essential role of the pastor in leading the congregation through tumultuous times, amid political leaders, philosophers, and heretics that are pulling the people of God in many different directions.

Chapter four considers his view of the human person, living under the transcendence and providence of God within the world God has created. I discuss the nature of the human person, which comprises both body and soul but also requires the indwelling of the Spirit. I explain the essential concepts of the image and likeness of God as the bookends for the spiritual life; the whole human person, created body and soul in the image of God, is conformed to the likeness of God and fitted for beholding the glory of God. Finally, I discuss the concepts of recapitulation and resurrection that guide Irenaeus' economic view of human growth and maturity. Together, these theological perspectives lead to his vision of beatitude where the faithful are raised to new life and fitted for immortality.

Then, chapter five considers Irenaeus' vision of Christian citizenship and political theology. I show how his doctrine of God and doctrine of creation framed his vision of public life. Irenaeus believes God has appointed earthly rulers with a measure of authority to accomplish some specific things. Magistrates perform God's work by enacting laws that curtail sin and justly delving out blessings and curses. The magistrates will also be judged accordingly in the way that they rule. Under every and any political rule, Irenaeus calls the Christian to a virtuous life that produces the most virtuous citizens.

Chapter six brings all things together in a discussion of what I call the apologetic life. In Irenaeus' day, the spiritual life was an apologetic life oriented toward discernment of truth amid error and the good life amid other competing visions. This discussion considers his depiction of the "spiritual disciple," who lives a discerning life and who judges all things and is judged by no one. I explain that the apologetic life is a life of fortitude and holiness, as well as discernment and persuasion.

Together these chapters show how Irenaeus and his community lived Christianly in a pagan world. Irenaeus was "zealous for the covenant of Christ" and, like many in his community, prepared the people of God to defend the faith, even to the end. The examples of these martyrs from Irenaeus' community reflect stories of faithfulness, and I pray that the church today is inspired to model this same kind of commitment.

1

ENGAGING CULTURE

Irenaeus lived in a tumultuous age that some might say is not that different from our own. Unlike people in later centuries, he did not enjoy the benefits of living in a Christendom, where the mores of the culture bore a Christian mark. He lived in a pagan Roman world with a patchwork of religious and philosophical communities that were vying for cultural real estate. This cultural competition is why the second century "was the century for the construction of Christian identity."[1] Christians such as Irenaeus had to formulate their beliefs and practices in conversation with a diverse group of other religious and philosophical communities. Throughout the empire, Christians gathered in groups that even the non-Christians recognized as being bound together as the "Great Church" and united in a common view of life.[2] These ancient Christians embraced an apologetic life, striving to demonstrate how the teachings of Christ are better and more fulfilling.

Irenaeus mentions principally interacting with three communities: Jews, philosophers, and Gnostics. In different ways, each of these groups shaped his theological reflections.

---

1. Donovan, *One Right Reading?*, 3.
2. Behr, *Identifying Christianity*, 9.

His interactions with Jews refined his interpretation of Scripture and his understanding of the person and work of Christ. Jews and Christians have a common source of revelation, but not a common hermeneutic. The pagan philosophers, on the other hand, start from reason not revelation and so challenged Irenaeus to clarify the relationship between faith and reason in his theological method. There is diversity of the philosophical schools, which offer a convenient contrast to the unity of the apostolic tradition. Finally, the Gnostics are his primary interlocutors. Irenaeus provides detailed analysis of the various Gnostic streams that pose an immediate threat to his community. In different ways, these groups provide counterpoints to Irenaeus' theological perspective which help bring his own thought into relief.

Engaging Jews

As the Christian church expanded during the first and second centuries, there was a steady parting of the ways between Christianity and Judaism. Texts such as Justin Martyr's *Dialogue with Trypho*, a stylized conversation between the Christian Justin and a Hellenistic Jew named Trypho that Eusebius reports took place in Ephesus, exemplify this religious parting.[3] Justin believed everything pointed to Christ, but his Jewish interlocutor, Trypho, refused to recognize him as the Messiah. Irenaeus was probably aware of Justin's dialogue, or at least the theological and exegetical arguments Justin makes.[4] Irenaeus makes similar moves in his writings, and the Old Testament texts, which Irenaeus clearly believes are inspired, offer common ground.[5] This liturgical performance of the Scriptures within Jewish life and practice provided a basis for apologetic conversations;

---

3.   Eusebius, *History of the Church*, 4.18. Justin Martyr, *Dialogue with Trypho*.

4.   Michael Slusser, "How Much Did Irenaeus Learn from Justin?" *Studia Patristica* 40 (2006), 515-20.

5.   He defends the inspiration of the Septuagint. See *Haer* 2.22.3; *Haer* 3.21.1-2.

Irenaeus notes that the Jews were "used to listen[ing] to Moses and the Prophets."[6] But in Irenaeus' view, the "writings of Moses speak of Christ," and even the Lord declared to the Jews, "If you believed Moses, you would believe me also, for he wrote of me."[7] Below I explain some of these moves, including his interpretation of Scripture and perspective on the Law.

Irenaeus argues that the Law functions in two ways for the Jews: discipline and prophecy. In Irenaeus' words, the Law was "both a training for them and a prophecy about future things."[8] In the first sense, the Jews had a course of discipline, or a way of life that was framed through the Decalogue. In the beginning God desired to bestow his blessings upon his creatures because, as Irenaeus writes, "man's glory is this: to persevere and remain in God's service."[9] So in order that the people of God might remain in relationship with God, God admonished the Jews through these "natural precepts that he had given and implanted in men from the Beginning," so that they might walk in God's ways.[10] The Jews were instructed "not to commit adultery, nor fornication, nor theft, nor fraud; and that whatsoever things are done to our neighbors' prejudice, were evil, and detested by God."[11] God also imposed upon the people other conditions of worship including: "the construction of the tabernacle, the building of the temple, the election of the Levites, sacrifices also, and oblations, legal monitions, and all the other service of the law" so that God's people, who were so prone to worship idols, would be instructed to serve God alone.[12]

---

6.   *Haer* 4.24.1.

7.   *Haer* 4.2.3.

8.   *Haer* 4.15.1.

9.   *Haer* 4.14.1.

10.   *Haer* 4.15.1.

11.   *Haer* 4.24.1.

12.   *Haer* 4.14.3.

All of these points of the Law, however, were of "secondary importance," as they were imposed to turn the hearts of the people to things of "primary importance."[13] The Law was given to the Jews, Irenaeus concludes, because of the hardness of their heart, so that they might turn their hearts to God.[14] He cites Moses' law of divorce as an example. Because the people of God were "stubborn" and not "submissive" to God's Law, Moses gave them the commandment of divorce.[15] Even the Law that was given to guide the people toward God has now been fulfilled in Christ. Originally, the Law was pedagogical, it had "an educational value," but after the work of Christ, freedom replaced servitude to the Law.[16] For the Jews the Law has its beginning and origin, but now in Christ, the Law has received "growth and the extension." Irenaeus writes of the fulfillment of the Law in a way that echoes the words of Christ in the Sermon on the Mount. "To assent to God, follow his Word," means that the people of God "love him above all things, and one's neighbor as oneself—man is man's neighbor—and...abstain from all evil activity."[17] Those in the church who follow the Word of God live in this way and in doing so, fulfill the Law.

Second, Irenaeus saw the Old Testament as prophecy that points to Christ. The Jews, Irenaeus writes, "apostatized from God, by not receiving his Word but thinking they can know the Father by himself without his Word, that is, without the Son."[18] When Jews read the Law it is like a "fable," because they do not understand the things in them that point to the Son of God.[19] Christians, on the other hand, see Christ everywhere in the Old

---

13. *Haer* 4.14.3.
14. *Haer* 4.15.2.
15. *Haer* 4.15.2.
16. Osborn, *Irenaeus of Lyons*, 239.
17. *Haer* 4.13.4.
18. *Haer* 4.7.4.
19. *Haer* 4.26.1.

Testament; he is the "treasure which was hid in the field" of the prophets, who is pointed out by "types and parables."[20] While the prophecies about Christ were hard to understand before his advent, now after the incarnation they have a clear exposition. Anyone who reads the Scriptures carefully will find "symbolic meaning" in them that points to Christ.[21]

How did Irenaeus interpret Christ as a treasure in the field of the Scriptures? The examples are numerous, but here are just a few. Abraham was not concerned with his earthly kin; he followed the Word of God who called him and "travelled as a pilgrim with the Word that he might dwell as a citizen with the Word."[22] Abraham followed the Word of the Lord to sacrifice as well.[23] Abraham, "by virtue of his faith," offered us "his only-begotten and beloved son as a sacrifice to God, so that God in turn might have the good pleasure of offering his beloved and Only-begotten Son for his [Abraham's] entire offspring as a sacrifice for our redemption."[24] In Genesis 27:28-29 Isaac prays that God may give to Jacob the "dew of heaven and of the fatness of the earth and plenty of grain and wine."[25] He also prays that many will serve Jacob, and that nations will bow down to him. From Irenaeus' vantage point, this passage must be fulfilled in Christ, because Jacob never experienced these things. Anyone who does not interpret the blessings of Jacob as referring to Christ, Irenaeus reasons, falls into "contradiction and opposition."[26] The Word also proclaimed to Moses, "I have surely seen the affliction of My people in Egypt, and I have

20.   *Haer* 4.26.1.

21.   *Haer* 4.26.1.

22.   *Haer* 4.5.3.

23.   *Haer* 4.5.4.

24.   *Haer* 4.5.4.

25.   *Haer* 5.33.3. All translations of *Against Heresies 5* are taken from: Irenaeus, *Against the Heresies; Books 4 and 5,* translated by Dominic J. Unger and Scott D. Moringiello, Ancient Christian Writers 72 (New York: Newman Press, 2024).

26.   *Haer* 5.33.3.

come down to deliver them."[27] In the Exodus account, Irenaeus understands that the Son of God is one who destroyed Amalek when Moses spread his hands and, in a similar way the Son saved the people "from the bite of the serpent by faith in him."[28] From these passages and others, the apostles showed how he "suffered whatsoever the prophet had predicted, and that He was the Son of God, who gives eternal life to men."[29]

Some Jews found the Christological argument persuasive. At one point, Irenaeus points to accounts of Jewish conversion in the New Testament, such as the example of Philip in the conversion of the Ethiopian Eunuch in Acts 8, and argues that the Jews were more easily persuaded to believe in Christ because they had read the Old Testament. When Philip found him traveling, the eunuch was reading Isaiah 53 and asked him about the passage. From that passage Philip showed him Christ in the Scriptures. This encounter exemplifies the shared authorities and the habit of reading Scripture that supported early Christian evangelistic efforts. Since the Eunuch has already received the Scriptures as authoritative, he was prepared for baptism because he "had been catechized in advance by the Prophets" and because he was only unaware of the "coming of God's Son."[30] He only needed to confess Christ and understand the new calling upon his life to understand what was written by the prophets. There was no great effort in the evangelization, because he was already "prepared in the fear of God by the prophets."[31]

Besides Philip, Irenaeus observes that other New Testament passages speak of mass conversions. The apostles "persuaded a great multitude" and "in one day, baptized three, and four, and five thousand men" because they already "possessed the

---

27. *Haer* 4.7.4.

28. *Haer* 4.23.2. Exod. 17:8-16 and Num. 21:4-9.

29. *Haer* 4.23.2.

30. *Haer* 4.23.2.

31. *Haer* 4.23.2. See also *Haer* 3.12.15.

fear of God."[32] They did more "readily receive the First-begotten from the dead, and the Prince of life of God."[33] What Irenaeus appreciated about the Jews was the simple fact that they enjoyed a shared authority. They had received the Old Testament and were following God, but they had rejected the Son of God and because of this rejection were no longer good interpreters of the promises of God. All of these points worked together so that there was fertile ground for his conversations with the Jews.

Engaging Philosophy

Alongside his comments on the Jews, Irenaeus has much to say about the Gentiles, especially the Greco-Roman philosophers with whom he interacted. Irenaeus is aware of the various philosophical traditions represented in his community, and uses philosophy with discernment; he will, for example, appeal to pagan sayings, works, or stories such as Aesop's fables and the story of Oedipus.[34] Of course, there are many different philosophical streams flowing in different directions like tributaries, each one characterized by different intellectual assumptions.

The Gnostic communities, which I will discuss next, also grow in the fertile soil of the philosophers. They absorb their ideas and construct theological systems with religious layering. Irenaeus recognizes that the philosophers are the intellectual basis for many heretical sects.[35] They sew together the scattered thoughts of the philosophers and craft a system that is worthless because it has been "patched together from old opinions, redolent of ignorance and irreligion."[36] They model their questions and answers after Aristotle and rely upon the thinking

---

32. *Haer* 4.23.2.

33. Haer 4.24.1.

34. Osborn, *Irenaeus of Lyons*, 33. See *Haer* 2.11.1; 2.14.1-9; 5.13.2.

35. *Haer* 2.14. All translations of *Against Heresies* 2 are taken from: Irenaeus, *Against the Heresies: Book 2*, translated by Dominic J. Unger and John J. Dillon, Ancient Christian Writers 65 (New York: Newman Press, 2012).

36. *Haer* 2.14.2.

of Plato, the Cynics, Epicurus, Pythagoras, or Democritus.[37] Some of the Gnostics even possess images of these philosophers that they honor and revere.[38]

Take the Valentinians. Irenaeus argues that they try to pass off the ideas of the comic poets and others philosophers who are "ignorant of God" as their own ideas.[39] He calls their view a patchwork of philosophical reflections that mask as a theological system, which they sew "together into a kind of cento out of many and worst rags, and so, by a subtle style, they prepare for themselves a fictitious cloak."[40] In other words, the whole basis for the Gnostic systems is the Greek mind that relies upon intellectual observation and sophistication to derive the principles of life.

But Irenaeus adds that some philosophers, such as Plato, are more religious than the Gnostics because they hold some theological perspectives that approach a true vision of God. Even Plato "acknowledged that the one and same God is both just and good and has power over all things, and even exercises judicial power."[41] He cites the words of Plato as evidence: "And God indeed, as also the ancient word has it, possesses the beginning and end and middle of all beings; he accomplishes [all things] justly, dealing with them according to their nature. But retributive justice against those who defect from the divine law always follow him."[42] He cites another Platonic saying that depicts the Maker and Framer of the universe as good and defines the "good" as "no jealousy even arises with regard to anything." This, in Irenaeus' reading, supports his doctrine of God, since the goodness of God

---

37. *Haer* 2.14.3–5; *Haer* 2.32.2; *Haer* 1.1.1.

38. *Haer* 1.25.6.

39. *Haer* 2.14.2.

40. *Haer* 2.14.2.

41. *Haer* 3.25.3.

42. *Haer* 3.25.3.

is "the beginning and the cause of the creation of the world."[43] These points are closer to Christian revelation than anything the Gnostic sects fabricate. Plato, not the Gnostics, offers a closer approximation of the Christian revelation.

But Irenaeus also observes that their philosophical systems contradict each other. There is no unity, just an endless cycling of new insights and observations that have no stability in some kind of coherent intellectual system. The philosophers produce "explanations that anyone excogitates," so there will be as many interpretations of truth as there are philosophers to provide them, and, more importantly, these truths will be "at war with each other and setting up contradictory opinions."[44] Irenaeus is happy to engage philosophical ideas; for example, he is critical of Plato's teaching on the transmigration of the souls because he believes it contradicts a Christian vision of the human person.[45] But engaging the philosophical tradition is not his main purpose; he only means to undermine the philosophical traditions from which the Gnostics draw.

Irenaeus' conversations with the philosophical streams have a different starting place based upon different sources than his conversations with Jews. His discussions of philosophical sources involve the nature of truth and the relationship between faith and reason. For the philosophers, all inquiry is rational inquiry. They have no sacred texts containing divine revelation that serve as the basis for knowledge. They trust their own minds. He sees fundamental differences between the way that the philosophers construct intellectual systems and the way the church expresses its faith. The plain sayings of the Scriptures help give order to life and thinking, such as the nature of God and the revelation of Christ. This is what he will term the rule of truth, or the rule of faith. These plain sayings provide a rule of truth that helps

---

43. *Haer* 3.25.3.
44. *Haer* 2.27.1.
45. *Haer* 2.33.1–6.

order knowledge, but there is no such rule of truth among the philosophers. Irenaeus argues that a "sound mind" is a mind "devoted to piety and the love of truth" and which "mediates upon the revelation of the Scriptures." A sound mind does not ignore any revelation available anywhere but instead reads that revelation through Scripture. Unless God is the first principle, the highest all-embracing reality, then the human mind is left with nothing but an infinite regress of unending worlds, gods, and philosophical views.[46]

Irenaeus notes that those who preached to the Gentiles did so "without the instruction from the Scriptures."[47] Given these differences Irenaeus argues, citing the book of Acts, that evangelization among the Gentiles is actually harder than among the Jews. He compares the story of the Philip mentioned above and the conversion of the Ethiopian Eunuch with Paul's mission to the Gentiles. In 1 Corinthians 15:10, Paul reports that he "worked harder than any of them," arguing that Gentile conversion required a more involved process of catechesis, both in terms of length and content. Those who minister among the Gentiles need to take things back to first principles and answer some fundamental questions such as: "how many gods are there?" or "what is the relationship between God and creation?"

Persuasion in these doctrines was not instantaneous. Irenaeus writes that Paul had to begin his instruction with the rejection of idolatry. Gentiles had to be convinced first to monotheism from polytheism, from the "superstition of idolatry" to "worship one God, the Creator of heaven and earth, and the maker of the entire creation."[48] They had to be convinced that "there is one God, who is above all principality, and dominion, and power, and every name which is named."[49] Then from that

---

46. Osborn, *Irenaeus of Lyons*, 34.

47. *Haer* 4.24.1.

48. *Haer* 4.24.1.

49. Eph. 1:21

point, they must see that the Word of God, who was with the Father from the beginning, became incarnate and accomplished salvation for all who confess faith in him. They must believe that "His Word, invisible by nature, was made palpable and visible among men, and did descend to death, even the death of the cross; also, that they who believe in Him shall be incorruptible and not subject to suffering, and shall receive the kingdom of heaven."[50] These points are expressions of the church's rule of faith that Irenaeus argues was confessed at baptism. He does not explain the rhetorical moves he would make, but surely some of these are represented in his extant works, *Against Heresies* and *Demonstration of the Apostolic Preaching.* In these cases, Irenaeus appeals to Scripture, but he also uses reason and natural law as the basis for their conversations. He goes so far as to claim that the "faith of the Gentiles is proved to be of a more noble description, since they followed the word of God without the instruction [derived] from the [sacred] writings."[51] The struggle to persuade Gentiles refined their faith and seasoned it with fortitude, so that those "who preached among the Gentiles underwent greater labor."[52]

Engaging Gnostics

Finally, between the Jews and the Gentiles, Irenaeus finds himself struggling with the Gnostics. They are much more of an immediate threat to his ministry, as some of the Gnostic groups have managed to persuade members of his community. The Gnostics are a sly bunch who worm their way into the homes of people, likely the wealthy ones, and try to deceive them with their crafty teaching. "By cleverness with words they persuasively allure the simple folk to this style of searching," Irenaeus writes, but then they "bring them to perdition by trumping up their

---

50. Phil. 2:8.

51. *Haer* 4.24.2.

52. *Haer* 4.24.2.

blasphemous and impious opinion against the Creator."[53] As Irenaeus sees it, these Gnostics are not just bad apples; they have a completely different conception of reality that shapes their moral life in dramatic ways. "By specious argumentation, craftily patched together," he writes, "they [Gnostics] mislead the minds of the more ignorant and ensnare them by falsifying the Lord's words."[54] In other words, they twist the Scriptures and conform them to a separate reality, a separate vision of life. The Gnostic interpretation of Scripture brings "many to ruin by leading them, under the pretense of knowledge, away from something more sublime and excellent to manifest than the God who made heaven and...all things in them."[55] The Gnostics are not satisfied with God; they long for their own knowledge and wisdom that transcends the one true God.

What did these Gnostics believe? Below I offer a brief explanation of Gnosticism, then focus on the Valentinian system, one of Irenaeus' key opponents, and finally explain two key apologetic arguments that Irenaeus cycles back to time and again: their interpretation of Scripture and their morality.

What is Gnosticism?

We know that Irenaeus had direct conversations with some Gnostics. Irenaeus tells us "after chancing upon the commentaries of the disciples of Valentinus—as they style themselves—and after conversing with some of them and becoming acquainted with their doctrine," he decides to write to his friend to help reveal the nature of these religious groups.[56] Part of the problem is that there are many different streams of Gnostics that interconnect but fan out in different directions like the branches of a tree. Nevertheless, they all share features and myths that bear a family

---

53.   *Haer* 1.pf.1.

54.   *Haer* 1.pf.1.

55.   *Haer* 1.pf.1.

56.   *Haer* 1.pf.2.

resemblance so that it is possible to generalize what most ancient Gnostics believed with a "typological model" that frames their basic convictions.[57]

First, Gnostics believe in "a completely other-worldly, distant, supreme God."[58] For the Valentinians the highest divine being is called the First-Father and this divine being has no association with anything material or earthly. Emanating from this being, there exists a hierarchy of divine beings, in different names, orders, and numbers, moving downward toward human creatures. These emanations create a plurality of divine figures existing in some remote, heavenly realm separate and distinct from the world, but gradually moving toward people.

Second, the Gnostics introduce a "distinct creator God or assistant," who is a lower aeon that creates the world. Typically, this lower being is called the Demiurge, which means "craftsman."[59] This Demiurge, moreover, is often described as ignorant, naive, evil, or with other such attributes that characterize his association with depraved things. The world this Demiurge created also bears the same attributes. So, the material world and all created things are by their very nature a depraved and evil creation.

Third, with these two elements in place, the distant aeons of the pleroma above, and the evil creation below, the Gnostics introduce some kind of mythological drama that explains how a "divine element" is, in various ways, implanted within some human beings and slumbers there.[60] They often divide humanity between those who are said to have the divine spark and those who do not. The Gnostics frequently appeal to the early chapters of Genesis to help explain this drama, but they

---

57. Christoph Markschies, *Gnosis: An Introduction* (New York: T&T Clark, 2003), 16–17.

58. Markschies, *Gnosis: An Introduction*, 16.

59. Markschies, *Gnosis: An Introduction*, 16–17.

60. Markschies, *Gnosis: An Introduction*, 17.

impose their conceptions of the Pleroma and Demiurge upon the text, dissecting it and conforming it to the realities above.

Fourth and finally, the "knowledge" ("gnosis" in Greek) of this myth and this state of affairs is gained through some "redeemer figure" from the Pleroma above who descends from that realm, imparts knowledge to some, and then return to it.[61] Those who receive the knowledge of the divine spark that resides within will find redemption when their spark is released from the body to ascend back to the Pleroma.

The essential theological assumption guiding this myth is a tendency toward dualism, meaning two opposing principles or entities that exist in conflict with each other. So, for example, there is a theological dualism between the perfect heavenly realm of aeons and the depraved earthly deities below. There is an anthropological dualism, a good divine spark that exists within some and an evil material body that opposes it. Other such dualisms continue in their view of the world.

But it is also challenging to catalog all the various Gnostic groups because they are constantly inventing new versions of this myth. Irenaeus admits that "it is difficult to describe all of their opinions" because they all "differ among themselves," and every day they "produce something that no one has ever thought of."[62] Irenaeus compares the evolving natures of the Gnostic myth to the spontaneous and annoying growth of mushrooms. A "multitude of Gnostics have sprung upon and shot out of the ground like mushrooms," he writes.[63] All of these groups are evolving and changing by adding new features to their myth.

The Valentinian Myth

The Valentinians, like the other Gnostic sects, have a unique version of the myth described above. Irenaeus explains their

---

61.   Markschies, *Gnosis: An Introduction*, 17.

62.   *Haer* 1.21.4.

63.   *Haer* 1.29.1.

myth in detail in *Against Heresies* 1-7 and mentions that his summary is based upon conversations with them and reading their books. He also knows of people among his congregation that have been persuaded by them.

The Valentinian system is not just some minor theological squabble with Irenaeus; it was an entirely different way of conceiving reality, a different view of the world. They begin describing the thirty aeons that dwell within the Pleroma, or "fullness," which is the Gnostic heavenly realm, and these aeons are bracketed into three groups and "enveloped in silence and are known to no one."[64] Only those who possess this secret knowledge can comprehend the mysteries of the spiritual realm. The highest and greatest being of this collection of deities is given different names, including "First-Being," "First-Beginning," "First-Father," and "Profundity." This First-Father, they argue, is characterized with many of the attributes that sound familiar to Christians. The First-Father is "incomprehensible and invisible, eternal and ingenerate, he existed in deep quiet and stillness through countless ages."[65] From this First-Father, other emanations flow downward and form the other beings, and all of these beings exist in congenial male and female pairs.

For the Valentinians, the First-Father has an extensive divine progeny with groups of philosophical and religious names, filling out the Pleroma. The First-Father deposited a seed into Silence, his partner, who brought forth Mind and Truth. Mind is also called "Only-Begotten," "Father," and "Beginning of all things." These four aeons (Profundity, Silence, Mind and Truth) are the four principle beings. From these four emanated four others: Word, Life, Man, and Church, which form the highest grouping aeons in the Pleroma. This grouping of eight is also called the "Ogdoad." From these other aeons come two other groups of aeons. One grouping of ten, termed the "Decad," consists of

---

64. *Haer* 1.1.3.

65. *Haer* 1.1.1.

the pairs: Profound, Mingling, Ageless, Union, Self-Producing, Pleasure, Immobile, Blending, Only-begotten, and Happiness. Then still lower is another grouping of twelve, or what is called the "Dodecad," consisting of Advocate, Faith, Paternal, Hope, Maternal, Love, Praise, Understanding, Ecclesiastic, Blessedness, Desired, and Wisdom.

From this theological reality, the Valentinians explain how the world was formed, how evil entered the world, and the destiny of those who come to a true understanding of things. Even among the Valentinians there are differences in their myths but, in general, they describe how Wisdom, "the last and youngest Aeon," committed an egregious and sinful error through "passion" by trying to seek after the First-Father and comprehend his greatness. This foolish endeavor brought nothing but grief and anguish to Wisdom. Wisdom was excluded from the pleroma and fell further into her range of passions: grief, fear, and perplexity all enveloping her. At the same time, she was filled with the good desire to return to the Pleroma. From this dualism the things of this world were born.

The Demiurge, or the creator of the world as the Valentinians argue, originated from Wisdom's evil passions, as did the world along with all other material substances. In Irenaeus' words, "From her [Wisdom's] amendment every soul of the world and of Demiurge took its origin; but from her fear and grief, all other things had their beginning."[66] In other words, the immaterial things that are eternal and redeemable are able to return, while the material and earthly are condemned and evil. Torn between these passions, when Wisdom would laugh and dwell upon returning to the heavenly realm the immaterial substance would emerge, but when she experienced fear and grief the material substance would come.

Finally, the formation and destiny of human beings fills out the Valentinian myth. Human beings, Valentinians teach, exist

---

66. *Haer* 1.4.2.

in three substances, "one out of passion, the material substance; the other out of amendment, the ensouled substance; the third, which she herself conceived, the spiritual substance."[67] These three substances have different fates: the material that will go to perdition, the spiritual that will ascend, and the ensouled that exists between them and "will go over to that element to which it has an inclination."[68] These three classes of people, which they term "Cain, Able, and Seth," have different destinies depending upon their internal natures: the "earthly indeed goes into corruption; but the ensouled, if it chooses the better things, will rest in the intermediate region; if, however, it chooses the worse things, it too will go to regions similar [to the worse things]."[69] They also "dogmatize that the spiritual people whom Achamoth had planted as 'seeds' from then until now in just souls, and which have been disciplined and nourished here below—because they were sent forth immature—and have finally become worthy of perfection."[70] So, the divine spark that slumbers within the spiritual class is, through their existence in the world, patiently disciplined to ascend back to the heavenly places. Some might wonder why anyone would find the Gnostic worldview appealing. For some, Gnosticism addressed the problem of evil, explaining the origins of good and evil and how evil would eventually be destroyed.

Scripture and Morality in Gnosticism

Irenaeus refutes several features of the Gnostic myth, beginning with their doctrine of God and their account of creation. As he often says, they invent a different god who is the mere figment of their imagination. But Irenaeus identifies some fundamental problems with the Gnostic myth in their biblical

---

67.　*Haer* 1.5.1.

68.　*Haer* 1.6.1.

69.　*Haer* 1.7.5.

70.　*Haer* 1.7.5.

interpretation and their moral perspective. The Gnostics try to validate their system by appeals to Scripture, which confuses and deceives those who are unfamiliar with Scripture. He also points to their problematic morality downstream from their theological perspective.

First, Irenaeus often characterizes the Gnostics as mishandling Scripture. They are "evil interpreters," "perverters and abusers of Scripture," and often found "garbling the Scriptures."[71] The Gnostics come with the myth described above and look for various ways that texts cohere to this system. In doing this, Irenaeus argues that "they disregard the order and the connection of the Scriptures, and so far as in them lies, dismember and destroy the truth."[72] "By transferring passages, dressing them up anew, and making one thing out of another, they succeed in deluding many through their wicked art in adapting the oracles of the Lord to their opinions."[73] He compares their interpretation of Scripture as that of persons who "patch together old wives' fables," stories that are just strung together haphazardly like "braiding a rope of sand."[74] Tying together the Scriptures with the myth mentioned above will not yield a stable structure. The reason they do this, Irenaeus contends, is so that their myths have "an air of probability": maybe people will believe this silliness if they cite Scripture. This practice deceives those who are unable to discern truth from error. For those who are not skilled in theological and philosophical discourse, the Gnostics "speak the same language we [Christians] do, but intend different meanings."[75] They use the words of Scripture to conform and deceive, and redeploy the Scriptures into a separate myth.

---

71. *Haer* 1.pf.1; 1.3.6; 2.pf.1. See also *Haer* 1.8.1; 1.9.1; 1.19.1–2.

72. *Haer* 1.8.1.

73. *Haer* 1.8.1.

74. *Haer* 1.8.1.

75. *Haer* 1.pf.2.

The Gnostic myth helps explain Irenaeus' famous mosaic image, which captures the way Gnostics misuse Scripture:

> Their [Gnostic's] manner of acting is just as if one, when a beautiful image of a king has been constructed by some skillful artist out of precious jewels, should then take this likeness of the man all to pieces, should rearrange the gems, and so fit them together as to make them into the form of a dog or of a fox, and even that but poorly executed; and should then maintain and declare that this was the beautiful image of the king which the skillful artist constructed, pointing to the jewels which had been admirably fitted together by the first artist to form the image of the king, but have been with bad effect transferred by the latter one to the shape of a dog, and by thus exhibiting the jewels, should deceive the ignorant who had no conception what a king's form was like, and persuade them that that miserable likeness of the fox was, in fact, the beautiful image of the king.[76]

The Gnostic interpreters desecrate the art of Scripture; they take the tiles or the tesserae and refashion them according to the myth that they present. The image they portray is a fox or a dog, some kind of image that portrays their craftiness, and an ugly one at that, a poor depiction of the truth of the Scriptures.

Some examples of exegesis will be helpful to understand Irenaeus' argument. After describing the Valentinian system, complete with the thirty aeons emanating downward from the First-Father, Irenaeus explains how they see this collection of divine beings in the Scriptures. They turn to passages such as the parable of the laborers that were sent into the vineyard.[77] If you add up all the hours of the mentioned in the passage (first, third, sixth, ninth, and eleventh hour), it totals to thirty. These mysteries, according to the Valentinians, "are great and wonderful and unutterable mysteries" that are only discerned

---

76. *Haer* 1.8.1.

77. *Haer* 1.1.3.

with the special knowledge of the myth. Like the parable of the laborers, the Valentinians look for anything else in that they can "adopt and accommodate to their baseless speculations."[78]

As to the formation of the Demiurge, the God of the Old Testament is another good example. To understand how the Gnostics read Scripture, its essential to see that the god depicted in the writings of the Old Testament is most often identified with the evil Demiurge. This means that the Gnostic reading tends to interpret every action of the God of the Old Testament as the action of an ignorant and depraved being that will ultimately be destroyed. The best example of the apparent foolishness of the Old Testament God is his claim, "I am God...and besides me there is no one."[79] This passage captures the arrogance and ignorance of the Demiurge who remains unaware that there is a collection of greater beings above him. The creator of the world, the God of the Old Testament, was ignorant even of his own mother, but instead foolishly imagined he alone was God. The Demiurge "made the heavens, without knowing the heavens; he fashioned man, without knowing Man; he brought the earth to light without understanding the Earth."[80] For the Gnostics, the God of the Old Testament is a foolish and stupid God who is "incapable of recognizing any spiritual essences."[81]

Second, given this theological system described above, what are the moral implications? If materiality is bad and they are merely spiritual beings—and only some of them at that—there is a natural tendency toward elitism, extreme asceticism, and immoral behavior. "Because of this doctrine," Irenaeus writes referring to their three-fold anthropology "the most perfect among them shamelessly do all the forbidden things, about which the

78.   *Haer* 1.1.3.

79.   *Haer* 1.5.4; 1.29.4; 1.30.6; 2.9.2. Versions of this phrase are cited in many passages such as: Deut. 32:39, Isa. 45:5, or Isa. 46:9.

80.   *Haer* 1.5.3.

81.   *Haer* 1.5.4.

Scriptures give guarantee that those who do such things shall not inherit the kingdom of God."[82] The Valentinians, for example, argue that "they are spiritual, not by conduct, but by nature."[83] Being spiritual by nature means that the "earthly element" cannot partake of salvation, while the spiritual element "cannot take on corruption, regardless of what practices they may have engaged in."[84] Irenaeus uses the image of a hunk of gold deposited in the mud to explain a Gnostics anthropology. Just as the gold, even when surrounded by mud, does not lose its beauty nor change its nature, the spiritual element is in no way affected by the muddy body. The spiritual element always preserves its nature, no matter what practices it partakes in.

This kind of anthropological dualism leads into two directions, either toward extreme asceticism, where the spiritual element tries to master the body, or extreme licentiousness, where the spiritual is unaffected by any immoral activity. The Gnostics maintain that they must have experience with every sort of view and immoral behavior; they turn to "pleasures, lusts, and immoral acts."[85] Irenaeus lists some examples of these immoral practices:

> Food sacrificed to idols they eat without scruple, thinking they no way define themselves by it. And they are the first to assemble at every heathen festival held in honor of the idols for the sake of pleasure, with the result that some do not abstain even from the spectacle loathsome to God and men where men fight wild beasts and each other in homicidal fashion. Others give themselves to carnal pleasures immoderately...Some secretly defile those women who are being taught this doctrine by them....Some even publicly and without shame, took away from their husbands whatever women they loved passionately

---

82.   *Haer* 1.6.3.

83.   *Haer* 1.6.2.

84.   *Haer* 1.6.2.

85.   *Haer* 2.32.2.

and took them as their own wives. Others, finally, who in the beginning feigned to dwell in chastity with them as sisters, were exposed as time went on when the "sister" becomes pregnant by the "brother."[86]

Both the licentious and ascetic tendencies are evident. Some of the Valentinians absorb all the immorality of the Roman culture, embracing all the licentiousness of the games and feasts. They indulge in every fetish and vice that premediates these gatherings. They also do things in private with women they have seduced into joining their ranks. There are those who claim to be chaste, apparently valuing the ascetic life, but in reality they are hypocrites. They feign an ascetic life, but then seduce women behind closed doors.

Irenaeus apparently has firsthand experience at the testimony of some who have been seduced by the Gnostics and then joined the church, revealing what had been done to them in secret and other things that were common among the Gnostic communities.[87] These practices often involved religious rites and practices that mimicked Christian ones, such as baptism or the Eucharist. But these often evolved into practices that took advantage of people, especially women.[88] These people, Irenaeus continues, "indulge in other foul and godless practices, against which we guard ourselves because of the fear of God and do not sin in thought or word."[89] The people of God are commanded not to participate in these kinds of behaviors.

Conclusion

In the late Second Century, Irenaeus found himself struggling among the coordinated efforts of Jews, philosophers, and Gnostics, each, in different ways, offereing perspectives that

---

86.   *Haer* 1.6.3.

87.   *Haer* 1.6.3

88.   *Haer* 1.13.1–7. Donovan, *One Right Reading?* 44–45.

89.   *Haer* 1.6.4.

competed with the teachings of the church. His interactions with Jews involved theological and exegetical debates centering on the relationship between Christ and the Old Testament. While the Jews and Christians had a common source of revelation, they applied a different hermeneutic. In subsequent chapters, Irenaeus' reading of the Old Testament will surface in many places, but the Jewish reading could not accept his arguments for Christ as the fulfillment of the Law.

The philosophers were a different matter altogether. The pagan philosophers had no concern for either the Old or the New Testament and based their philosophical systems on reason. So, in his interactions with philosophy, Irenaeus had to backtrack to first principles and explain the relationship between faith and reason. Given that they start with reason and not revelation, there are a diverse number of philosophical schools of thought. In the church, Irenaeus argues, there is unity in the apostolic tradition derived from the Scriptures.

Finally, Irenaeus' primary apologetic efforts were aimed at the Gnostics. He remains an important sources for the history of the Gnostics and the ways that the church addressed their theological arguments. The Gnostics, along with the Jews and the philosophers, help bring Irenaeus' own thought into relief.

These groups show that Irenaeus' defense of the faith was not just a matter of differences of opinion on specific theological questions, but they were competing theological systems, or what amounts to different views of reality. In the next chapter, I begin explaining Irenaeus' theological system, which begins with his doctrine of God.

2

A THEOLOGICAL SYSTEM

When Irenaeus found himself engaging Gnostics and others, he knew that their disagreements went all the way down to their assumptions of first principles. They had very different conceptions of reality with very different visions of life. For Irenaeus, everything is downstream of God, the creator and sustainer of all things. In this chapter, I begin with Irenaeus' first principles, his theological system, which includes his doctrine of God and conviction that God is the source of all truth. Only when a person has a right view of God can he or she begin to conceive of the right perspective on the human person and the right vision of life. Those who affirm the true view of God will be able to understand the revelation given to God's people. Second, I explain the rule of faith. The rule is derived from the revelation of Scripture and forms a faithful summary of what Scripture teaches. The rule summarizes Irenaeus' theological vision that guides his spiritual life, like a set of spectacles through which Irenaeus sees all things. Third, I explain Irenaeus' theological method, including how the relationship between faith and reason demands an intellectual humility. Together these perspectives provide the theological basis for Irenaeus' spiritual life.

The First Principles of God

Irenaeus' doctrine of God participates in his basic perspective on the nature of truth. Irenaeus is committed to truth, but in his assessment truth corresponds to reality, or a description of "things truly real."[1] His logic goes like this: "faith is produced by the truth; for faith rests on things that truly are." This logic means that metaphysics—the branch of philosophy that deals with the nature of being, substance, cause, and identity—and other matters of first principles are the main focus of Irenaeus' theological project. True faith, in Irenaeus' reasoning, is dependent upon reality or things that truly exist, and only believing in "things that are, as they are," and keeping "firm our confidence in them."[2] Any quest for the basis of first principles, either by studying history or empirical evidence, would only substitute another first principle. Instead, as Behr argues, "'first principles' are always and in every case accepted on faith."[3]

Irenaeus' first principles, then, begin with the assumption that God is the fundamental source and foundation for everything. God is the starting place, the first principle, the unmoved mover. God precedes existence and all existence comes from God. For those who deny God, and thus maintain a materialist view of reality where the only object of reality is a material world, it might be hard to understand Irenaeus' conviction. He sees beyond the material to perceive the spiritual plane of reality that, in his mind, is the more fundamental to reality itself than only what we see, hear, touch, and taste.

Faith, then, is believing in what is truly real. Irenaeus writes, since "the conserver of our salvation is faith, it is necessary to take great care of it, that we may have a true comprehension

---

1. *Epid* 3. All translations of Irenaeus' Demonstration of the Apostolic Preaching are taken from: Irenaeus, *On the Apostolic Preaching*, translated by John Behr, Popular Patristics Series 17 (Crestwood, NY: St Vladimir's Seminary Press, 1997).

2. *Epid* 3.

3. Behr, *Identifying Christianity*, 11.

of what is."[4] Faith is produced from truth, which points to the reality of God's existence and the work of God over creation. For these are the things that "truly are." These are the things that the Christian believes exist and maintains a firm confidence in their reality. This is the "true" comprehension of things that exists as they exist. This faith is received and confessed at baptism before the people of God. We are saved by faith, trusting in God because things come from God and all things find their proper identity and formation in relation to God.

In the second century, Irenaeus must take things back to first principles and the discussion of God because philosophers and Gnostics deny the Christian view of God. Osborn argues that one of the key unifying assumptions of Irenaeus' project is the "universal Intellect," the being of God who holds all things together.[5] Given the Gnostic arguments, Irenaeus writes, "It is necessary, then, that we begin with the first and greatest principle, with the Creator God who made heaven and the earth and all things in them."[6] God is the creator of all things, and everything that has life and breath derives its existence from him. God "alone is God, and he alone is Lord, and he alone is Creator, and he alone is Father."[7] He alone, Irenaeus continues, "contains all things, and he himself gives existence to all things."[8] There is nothing higher or greater than God and no one can trace their origin to some other being or reality besides God.

Rejecting any argument that evolves into an infinite regress, Irenaeus argues that it is not possible for anything, any "Fullness, Beginning or Power or another God" to be above God. God contains all things and is contained by nothing.[9] If, as the

---

4.   Epid 3.

5.   Osborn, Irenaeus of Lyons, 21.

6.   Haer 2.1.1.

7.   Haer 2.1.1.

8.   Haer 2.1.1.

9.   Haer 2.1.2.

Gnostics and other heretics suppose, there is a higher god or Fullness or Being that encloses or contains god, there must also be a third Being that contains and encloses the second higher god. And following this reasoning, they speculate that these other gods above and below "would have a beginning in relation to some other beings; and this would go on forever, so that their speculation would never come to a stop in the one God."[10] There would be an infinite regress where every being depends upon the one who came before it. The various heretical groups Irenaeus encountered exemplify this principle. They all imagine different numbers of gods: for Marcion, for example, there are only two gods, but for the Valentinians there are thirty. Other groups conjure up a different number depending upon the ingenuity of their myth. But none of these beings would be God. Because each one would only possess "a very small portion in relation to the rest," denying divine omnipotence.[11] In this sense, Irenaeus argues that this infinite regress contradicts the God revealed in the Scriptures.

Irenaeus' view of God possesses all the classical attributes, including both the intrinsic and extrinsic attributes.[12] Two key attributes intrinsic to God, which surface regularly in his discussion of the heretics, are divine infinitude and simplicity.[13] God is the creator who made heaven and earth. He alone is God and encloses all things, but is enclosed by nothing, which is a "formulaic way of expressing that God is unlimited."[14] God's infinitude implies his transcendence, incomprehensibility, and immanence. God's creatures are weak and finite, prone to sin and depravity, but God's nature excels these things.[15] God is not

---

10. *Haer* 2.1.3.

11. *Haer* 2.1.5.

12. Osborn, *Irenaeus of Lyons*, 28.

13. Anthony Briggman, *God and Christ in Irenaeus* (Oxford: Oxford University Press, 2019), 71.

14. Briggman, *God and Christ in Irenaeus*, 75.

15. *Haer* 2.28.2.

like human beings; God's thoughts are not like human thoughts, God is all thought, lacking nothing.[16]

God is simple too. In Irenaeus' words, God is "simple and not composite; with all members of similar nature, being entirely similar and equal to him."[17] The Scriptures know of no other God; no revelation given to any prophet or apostle speaks of any other god beside the one and only true God. God alone is "all Mind, all Spirit, all Understanding, all Thought, all Word, all Hearing, all Eye, all Light, and the whole source of all blessing."[18] God's thoughts are not like human thoughts; God is "far removed from the actions and passions that men and women experience."[19] Human persons are "composite ensouled beings" so it is possible to speak, for example, of the difference between thought and speech.[20] Irenaeus illustrates: "the tongue, being fleshy, is not able to keep up with the speed of the human mind, which is spiritual; hence our word is held back within and is not instantaneously uttered as it was conceived by the mind, but piecemeal, as the tongue can minister to it."[21] God is not like this. God is simple. God is "all Mind, and all Word, what he thinks he speaks, and what is speaks he thinks."[22] God is "all intelligence, all spirit who is active, all light, and always existing the same and unchangeable."[23] To summarize all this, Irenaeus cites the words of Paul: "There is only One God, the Father, who is able all and throughout all and in us all."[24]

---

16. *Haer* 1.12.2; 4.19.3; 2.13.3.

17. *Haer* 2.13.3.

18. *Haer* 2.13.3.

19. *Haer* 2.13.3.

20. *Haer* 2.28.4.

21. *Haer* 2.28.4. Irenaeus observes that Greek thought identifies the Word as the directing power in the human person from the organ that utters the word.

22. *Haer* 2.28.5.

23. *Haer* 2.28.4.

24. *Haer* 2.2.4. Eph. 4:6.

Irenaeus also speaks of God's extrinsic attributes, those which emphasize God's economic activity among God's creation and creatures. Irenaeus speaks of God's work in the divine economy. God has made all things, through the Son and Spirit, as he willed, "bestowing on all things their form and order, and the principle of their creation."[25] All things include animals, humans, angels, everything has been fitted and prepared by God for God's purposes. The "harmony of creation" demonstrates that God has made things "well ordered" to God's purposes.[26] God's "whole economy," Irenaeus tells us, "tends toward salvation," and "His Word establishes all things and by His Wisdom harmoniously united them."[27] God's work of salvation is the abiding reminder "both what God is capable of and what benefit man receives, and so might not stray at any time from the true understanding of the things that exist just as they are, that is, those of God and of man."[28] Those who stray from the true comprehension of things reject reality, or the proper understanding of God and the true destiny of humanity according to God's purposes.

Rule of Faith

Irenaeus describes "truth" or "faith" in a statement of faith that he calls the "rule of truth" or the "rule of faith." The rule of truth is a summary of the deposit of faith confessed at baptism, that unifies the people of God and guides the faithful toward godliness. The two terms, rule of truth and rule of faith, refer to the same thing—a doctrinal summary of the apostolic teaching—but the different terms are used in different contexts. When Irenaeus speaks of his summary of Christian orthodoxy in the context of his apologetics against Gnostics, he calls it the "rule of

---

25. *Haer* 2.2.4.
26. *Haer* 2.15.3.
27. *Haer* 3.24.1; 3.24.2.
28. *Haer* 5.2.3.

truth."[29] It is a summary of the truth of God and the salvation that separates him from his Gnostic interlocutors. Since the Gnostics, or anyone else for that matter, do not know the true God, they do not know truth. Instead, their doctrines of god are received "as they were able to hear it," according to the various teachers who deliver new instruction. So outside the church, "no one would have the rule of truth, since all the disciple would credit their [teachers] with giving out speech according to the capacity of the one to understand and grasp it."[30] None of them learn truth from God, but instead, "by not thinking wisely, they convict themselves inasmuch as they do not agree on the same words" and have no fundamental agreement about first principles.[31] Or, as Irenaeus says elsewhere, since the Gnostics do not "possess the rule of truth," there will be as many interpretations of Scripture as there are persons attempting to explain them.[32]

But when Irenaeus articulates his summary of doctrine in his catechetical manual, he terms it the "rule of faith."[33] It is a summary of the truth confessed in faith by those in the church at baptism. Christians have faith in God, who is what is real and true, trusting in the one true God for all matters of life and practice. In the church, Christians follow the one true God and "possess his words as the Rule of Truth," so that in the church, as a matter of first principles, Christians "speak the same things always about the same passages," meaning that in the church, Christians know only "one God, the Creator of the universe."[34] Irenaeus challenges believers to hold "in himself the Rule of the Truth which he received by means of baptism."[35]

---

29.   *Haer* 1.9.4; 2.27.1; 3.11.1; 3.12.6; 3.15.1; 4.35.4.

30.   *Haer* 3.12.6.

31.   *Haer* 4.35.4.

32.   *Haer* 2.17.1.

33.   *Epid* 3; 6.

34.   *Haer* 4.35.4.

35.   *Haer* 1.9.4.

Patristics scholar J.N.D. Kelly describes the rule of faith as "a condensed summary" of the faith that is "fluid in its wording but fixed in content, setting out the key-points of the Christian revelation."[36] To speak of the rule as both "fluid" and "fixed" makes good sense for Irenaeus. Irenaeus refers to or summarizes the rule of faith in several places, and, while they are not identical, there is a "family resemblance" among them, such as the order of traits and characteristics shared by a biological family. Irenaeus will affirm that "the doctrine of the apostles" has handed down "a correct and harmonious explanation according to the Scriptures, without danger or blasphemy."[37] The "doctrine of the apostles" implies a whole system or a framework that transcends all Christian confessions. But, as the different expressions of the rule of faith in Irenaeus indicate, there are several different versions of this summary of faith.

This is similar to what the later tradition will identify as "the faith which is believed" (fides quae creditur), that is the body of faith expressed in doctrinal form, and which is contrasted with "the faith that believes" (fides qua creditur), or the personal faith that assents to the faith that is confessed.[38] The people of God share in these things, even if they do not always agree on secondary matters of faith and practice. Irenaeus uses the term "hypothesis," which I think captures the unity of the "faith which is believed," that is, the objective faith summarized in the rule. The rule of faith is like a single hypothesis that summarizes the faith.[39] The term hypothesis is a Greco-Roman term meaning "the presentation (sometimes in a summary) of a plot or structure intended by an author such as Homer."[40] Irenaeus

---

36. J.N.D. Kelly, *Early Christian Doctrines*, revised fifth edition (London: A&C Black, 1977; reprint Continuum, 2006), 37.

37. *Haer* 4.33.8.

38. Augustine makes this distinction in his work on the doctrine of the Trinity: Augustine, *On The Trinity*, 13.2.5.

39. Behr, *Identifying Christianity*, 11, 79.

40. Robert Grant, *Irenaeus of Lyons* (New York: Routledge, 1997), 53.

uses the illustration of a Homeric cento to do so. I have already spoken about the mosaic above that communicates a similar idea, but an ancient cento was a poem composed entirely of words from other literary sources. It's a patchwork of quotations drawn together to communicate some theme or idea. Irenaeus cites the example of a Homeric cento, which brings together an eclectic array of quotes from the *Iliad* and *Odessey*. The Gnostics, who often cite Scripture, do so without the rule of faith and, in so doing, "gather together sayings and names from scattered places" in the Scriptures and then twist them "from a natural meaning to an unnatural one."[41] Anyone who knows the writings of Homer will recognize that the verses were spoken by Ulysses, Hercules, Priam, Menelaus, or Agamemnon, and will place them back in their correct place and unmask the fabricated theme of the cento. In a similar way, anyone who confessed the rule of truth and holds fast to the rule will recognize when people, such as the Gnostics, misuse and misinterpret the Scriptures, applying them to their own fabricated system of truth.

Irenaeus does not provide a sanctioned version of the rule of faith that is affirmed by any ecclesial body, but he does provide versions of the rule of faith mingled with apologetic arguments.[42] Irenaeus is fine with this unity and diversity. He believed that God is ontologically prior to the rule, and so the rule is an attempt to explain God, or, used in polemical contexts, to refute points of doctrine that deviate from the rule. Diversity was, as Behr argues, "an integral element of its [the church's] catholicity."[43] But the notion of the aforementioned "family resemblance" suggests that there are some common features among his descriptions of the rule—even if the particular terms that comprise the wording of his rule vary with each summary. For a non-polemical version of the rule of faith we need to

---

41. *Haer* 1.9.4.

42. *Haer* 1.10.1; 1.22.1; 3.3.3; 3.11.1.

43. Behr, *Identifying Christianity*, 9.

turn to the *Demonstration*. This is the closest thing to an official version that would be confessed at baptism:

> And this is the order of our faith, the foundation of [the] edifice and the support of [our] conduct: God, the Father, uncreated, uncontained, invisible, one God, the Creator of all: this is the first article of our faith. And the second article: the Word of God, the Son of God, Christ Jesus our Lord, who was revealed by the prophets according to the character of their prophecy and according to the nature of the economies of the Father, by whom all things were made, and who, in the last times, to recapitulate all things, became a man amongst men, visible and palpable, in order to abolish death, to demonstrate life, and to effect communion between God and man. And the third article: the Holy Spirit, through whom the prophets prophesied and the patriarchs learnt the things of God and the righteous were led in the path of righteousness, and who, in the last times, was poured out in a new fashion upon the human race renewing man, throughout the world, to God.[44]

From this statement of the rule of faith, we can discern several features. First, in the opening line he characterizes the rule of faith with a variety of descriptors that indicate that the rule serves as a summary of first principles communicating the essence of the teaching of the apostles. The rule of faith, in the words of Irenaeus, is "the foundation of the building, and the consolidation of a way of life."[45] The rule of faith describes a Christian vision of that which is true, or of reality, the way that a Christian perceives God and the world. In introducing it Irenaeus stipulates the rule to be the "order" of our faith. In other words, it is the basic arrangement of theological truth given to the church. It emerges out of the Scriptures and formulates an organized summary of Christian doctrine. This order of faith is also the "foundation" of doctrine upon which the building of the church is constructed.

---

44. *Epid* 6.

45. *Epid* 6.

Second, the triune name in the command of Matthew 28:19—to go into the world "and make disciples of all nations, baptizing them in the name of the Father, and of the Son, and of the Holy Spirit" —serves as the outline for the rule of faith, which weaves together both the narrative of salvation history and the dogmatic claims of the faith under the triune name. These dogmatic claims are propositional statements, attributes, or ontological descriptors of the nature of God, such as the statement that God is "uncreated, uncontained, invisible, one God," as mentioned in the rule of faith. This included the true nature of God, the world, and the relationship of people to both. All theological and moral judgments depend upon the objective truth presented in the rule. The metaphysical assumptions of the rule inform their epistemology, or what they know to be ultimately true, and ethics, or how they are to live. Each name of the triune God provides a heading that helps explain the key points of the rule, meaning that Christology, the doctrine of Christ, and Pneumatology, the doctrine of the Spirit, are a seamless part of the rule, integrated within it. Irenaeus will make the link between baptism and the rule of faith explicit in several places. The people of God, Irenaeus writes, "have received baptism for the remission of sins, in the name of God the Father, and in the name of Jesus Christ, the Son of God, who was incarnate and died and rose again, and in the Holy Spirit of God."[46] Here, the allusion to Matthew 28:19 signals that basic rubric or outline of the rule of faith confessed at baptism.

The heart of the rule is Christ.[47] In (writing of, explaining, discussing, etc.) the rule of faith confessed at baptism, Irenaeus captures his vision of Christ that includes both the description of Christ's person and work, including his deity and humanity, as well as his economic activity, including Christ's preexistence, birth, death, resurrection, and Second Coming. Christ is the

---

46. *Epid* 3.
47. Behr, *Identifying Christianity*, 140.

Son of God and the Word of God, and through the Father he created all things. The Son of God was revealed by the prophets in the Old Testament "according to the character of their prophecy and according to the nature of the economies of the Father."[48] The Son of God became incarnate, becoming "a man amongst men...visible and palpable." In his person and work, Christ recapitulated all things in himself and abolished death, reestablishing "communion between God and man." The same kind of theological summary accompanies the Holy Spirit. The Spirit inspired the prophets of the Old Testament and led the people of God through the journey of salvation. In the New Covenant, the Spirit of God was poured out upon the people of faith, "renewing man throughout the world, to God."

Every point of doctrine is important, as the church is slowly explaining the work of Christ and the Spirit to new converts. There are many versions of the rule of faith because there are many different descriptors that one could give to God. Irenaeus himself offers several different versions of the rule that are shaped by the context, be it polemical or catechetical.

Third, the rule of faith articulates the preaching of the apostles, and it exists in dialectic relationship with Scripture. Every word or concept in the rule of faith is derived from some reference to the very wording of teaching in Scripture. The rule reflects the nature of God as proclaimed and handed down by those who conversed with the Lord. Describing the unity of the apostolic preaching of the church, Irenaeus writes that though the church is "disseminated throughout the whole world," nevertheless there remains doctrinal unity and continuity among all the churches.[49] For the universal church is like "one house" that has received the teaching of the apostles.[50] The church "believes these things as if she had but one soul

---

48. *Epid* 6.
49. *Haer* 1.10.1.
50. *Haer* 1.10.1.

and one and the same heart; she preaches, teaches, and hands them down harmoniously, as if she possessed but one mouth."[51] Irenaeus emphasizes the geographical unity of the faith of the universal church saying, "though the languages throughout the world are dissimilar, nevertheless the meaning of the tradition is one and the same. . . .The churches which have been founded in Germany do not believe or hand down anything else; neither do those founded in Spain or Gaul or Libya or in the central regions of the world."[52] But just as there is one sun that shines everywhere, so there is one God and one faith that shines upon the entire church. The people of God partake of the same Spirit, confessing the same rule of faith.

Finally, the rule of faith is integrated into the liturgical life of the church, reinforcing their basic convictions and guiding them in their lives, their worship, and all evangelistic and apologetic encounters. The rule is the "stability" for every conversation, which helps the Christian put all other philosophical claims and moral arguments into perspective.[53] The early church's right ordering of authorities, by contrast, made God the source of knowledge and the basis for truth and ethics. From that starting point the church built an ordered structure of knowledge and determined the right moral patterns. The rule describes how God created all things, and mentions the economies of God that contain creation, the coming of Christ, the Spirit, the church, and the Second Coming. With these claims, the rule helps guide what the church preaches, how the church worships, and the way the church relates to the world around it. Irenaeus implores Christians to "keep the rule of faith unswervingly and perform the commandments of God."[54] The rule is confessed at baptism, which also forms "the seal of eternal life and rebirth unto God,

---

51. *Haer* 1.10.1.

52. *Haer* 1.10.2.

53. *Epid* 6.

54. *Epid* 3.

that we may no longer be the sons of mortal men, but of the eternal and everlasting God."[55] The theological claims made here, which also assume the triadic structure of the rule of faith, means that in baptism, the Christian has received new birth and eternal life, and is no longer the son or daughter of "mortal men." Now they live in a world under the care of "the eternal and everlasting God" who has made all things and "everything is subjected to Him, so that God does not rule nor is Lord over what is another's, but over His own, and all things are God's."[56] Upon this summary of faith the people of God can order their lives, so that, whether surrounded by ancient stoics or modern secularists, this rule orders reality.

Theological Method

The discussion of the rule of faith introduces an important framework for thinking about Irenaeus' theological method, which situates a key relationship between faith and reason. The modern period is known for its elevation of reason at the expense of faith, but Irenaeus approaches things differently. As I discussed earlier, he is aware of the philosophers; Irenaeus knows that the Greek mind is capable of rational inquiry and understands that reason is a powerful authority to discern truth from error. But he does not trust that the mind is capable of understanding all things, especially not the mysteries of God. So, he believes that it is necessary to walk by faith, turning to God's revelation to guide us.

The first premise of Irenaeus' theological method is *faith seeking understanding.* This phrase is a classic definition of theology that finds clear exposition in Irenaeus' catechetical text. Citing Isaiah 7:9, Irenaeus argues: "Action, then, comes by faith, as 'if you do not believe,' Isaiah says, 'you will not understand.'"[57]

---

55. *Epid* 3.

56. *Epid* 3.

57. *Epid* 3.

But he also adds that "truth brings about faith, for faith is established upon things truly real."[58] Faith, then, is the basis for knowledge and the understanding of things as they exist. Irenaeus implores the Christians to maintain their faith, and to have a true comprehension of things as they are, and then he calls his readers to live under the assumption that faith informs their actions. This passage comes at the beginning of Irenaeus' catechetical work, which sets the paradigm for his biblical and theological instruction that continues throughout the rest of the work. The faith of the church provides a theological vision of life that helps make sense of everything else.

Second, Irenaeus believes all rational inquiry must begin with faith, because reason is part of God's economy. There is a proper ordering to knowledge that must be respected. In *Haer* 2.25–28, Irenaeus provides a summary of his theological method.[59] In Irenaeus' words, Christians must "keep order in your knowledge and, ignorant as you are of what is good, do not go beyond God himself; for no one can go beyond him."[60] Do not ignore God or assume any position of knowledge that attempts to explain reality as if God does not exist. Doing so would be trying to raise yourself above God, seeking explanations of things that do not involve God, trying to understand all things without God. In rhetorical fashion, Irenaeus reminds the reader, "For you, O man, are not increate, nor did you always exist along with God, as his own Word did"; instead, through God's goodness "you now begin to exist as a creature and gradually learn from the Word the economies of God who made you."[61] Human creatures always walk in faith in something, and Irenaeus implores them to walk in faith in the one true God; the God who made them. Keeping

---

58.   *Epid* 3.

59.   W. R. Schoedel, "Theological Method in Irenaeus (*Adversus Haereses* 2.25–28)," *The Journal of Theological Studies*, vol. 35, no.1 (1984), 31–49.

60.   *Haer* 2.25.4.

61.   *Haer* 2.25.4.

the "order of knowledge" means walking in faith, confessing the rule of faith.[62] The rule is, in this sense, a "system of truth" that orders and arranges all other things, because God does not derive from "created things," but "created things come from God."[63] Meaning that any rational inquiry into created things ought not to deny the God who created all things, including the mind that is reasoning.

Irenaeus warns those who rely upon their reason not to become puffed up by their own thinking and inclinations. They are creatures made by God and the only path forward is to use their minds to conceive of truth in relationship to God. He leans on Paul's warning in 1 Corinthians 8:1, "knowledge puffs up, but love builds up." Good theological method requires the virtue of humility. "Now, there is no greater conceit than to think that one is better and more perfect than he who created and formed us, and gave us the breath of life, and bestowed existence itself," Irenaeus writes.[64] There is no greater arrogance than the person who assumes that they conceive of truth without the aid of the very breath and mind that God gave them.

Irenaeus' theological method demands close attention to divine revelation. Those who are seeking truth are called to mediate upon the Scriptures. This brings us back to the ordering of faith and reason in Irenaeus' theological method. The person who possesses a "sound mind" is one who mediates upon the things God has given to humanity and placed within our reason. Irenaeus stresses the right use of the mind, saying, "The sound and safe and religious and truth-loving mind will readily apply itself to the things God placed within the power of men and granted to our knowledge."[65] The one who applies his or her mind to the things of God through "daily exercise," will easily

---

62. *Haer* 2.25.4.

63. *Haer* 2.25.1.

64. *Haer* 2.26.1.

65. *Haer* 2.27.1.

acquire the knowledge of God and the world.[66] The most plain and unambiguous things are set forth in the Scriptures. There are many things to investigate and many things that come within the grasp of our knowledge. But the most sure and true knowledge comes to us in the Scriptures; "the Scriptures are perfect, inasmuch as they were given by God's Word and Spirit."[67] We are able to comprehend the plain statement of Scripture, the revelation of the nature of God, the clear exposition of creation and the formation of humanity, and the revelation of the Son in the proclamation of the apostles. All point to the basic elements of the rule of faith.

There is truth revealed in nature which is accessible to the rational mind; but much of it, Irenaeus contends, is confounding and so must be left in the hands of God. Irenaeus gives many examples of rational inquiry into such natural phenomenon as the rising of the Nile, the migration of birds, the ebb and flow of the oceans, the changing weather patterns, the waxing and waning of the moon, and the sources and origins of different types of waters, rocks, minerals, and metals. "While trying to find the causes of such things we can really be loquacious," Irenaeus writes, "yet God alone, who made them, can tell the truth."[68] We may be able to say much about the natural causes and present many plausible theories or solutions, but there are limits to human understanding. But not to God who formed and made all these things; God is omniscient. God has ordained things in this way so that God would always be teaching and humanity would always be learning. Not only in the present age, but even in the age to come.[69] Above all things, and possessing "the Rule of Truth itself and the manifest testimony about God," Irenaeus

66. *Haer* 2.27.1.

67. *Haer* 2.28.2.

68. *Haer* 2.28.2.

69. *Haer* 2.28.3.

writes, "we ought not to cast out the solid and true knowledge about God by running from one solution to another."[70]

Those who maintain this proper ordering of knowledge, with faith seeking understanding, viewing all things through the rule of faith, and leaving those things that are unknown in the hands of God, then, Irenaeus concludes, that all scriptural revelation will harmonize and point toward a system of truth, so that "through the many voices of the passages there will be heard among us one harmonious melody that hymns praises to God who made all things."[71]

Conclusion

Contrary to the culture surrounding him, Irenaeus was confident in the revelation given by God. He trusted that God is the source of all truth, and this formed the first principles of his theological method. Only those who have a right view of God can understand the Scriptures and discern the right vision of life. Irenaeus summarizes his first principles, or his doctrine of God, in his rule of faith. The rule of faith and Scripture exist in a dialectic relationship, as the church is always addressing theological challenges and formulating theology in conversation with cultural authorities. The rule is a summary of his theological views and functions like a set of spectacles through which Irenaeus sees all things. In this way the rule also helps explain his theological method, which demands an intellectual humility and begins with the premise of faith seeking understanding. While there are many perplexing things in creation, the only sure and true knowledge is the knowledge of God From the existence of God, the believer can make sense of everything else, including the right way to live. The pastor has a pivotal role in helping guide people in this theological vision of God, and this idea is the topic of the next chapter.

---

70. *Haer* 2.28.1.

71. *Haer* 2.28.3.

3

PASTORAL MINISTRY

During his years of ministry, Irenaeus encountered the competing visions of life described in the previous chapters. The Jews, philosophers, and Gnostics, among other groups, offered different paths to walk. To help navigate these realities, Irenaeus offers a Christian worldview, a way of life that runs alongside but contrary to these assumptions and remains faithful to the theological vision of the rule of faith. As a pastor, Irenaeus worked to encourage his people and his readers to embrace the counter-cultural spiritual life, a way of living that was able to navigate the ditches and dangers of the culture, while at the same time living as a faithful citizen in the world.

In his writings, Irenaeus cast a vision of pastoral ministry that would help encourage Christians to pursue the spiritual life. In this chapter, I turn to his role as pastor and church leader, explaining how Irenaeus viewed ministry. First, the two qualities of a good pastor are sound teaching and blameless conduct. Like two hands, these two features work together to guide pastoral care. The pastor should be skilled in discerning truth and an exemplar in virtue, prepared to lead God's people in wisdom. These two features are the decisive characteristics of remaining faithful to the apostolic teaching. What does it mean to be in the line of the apostles? It means teaching in accordance with the apostolic teaching and living a holy life that conforms to that teaching. Second, I discuss the importance of the sacraments of baptism and the Eucharist. Just as sound teaching of the Word of God is one feature of the pastor's calling, so is the administration of the sacraments. These features of the spiritual life help orient the worship of the church and guide the people of God toward salvation. Finally, I discuss a few other key features of the spiritual life of the church including prayer and martyrdom. For Irenaeus and his community, prayer was an indispensable feature of the spiritual life. Martyrdom was also an abiding concern and shaped how the people conducted themselves in the community. Irenaeus views all these features of ministry as essential for the life of the church in the ancient world. He sees the essential role of the pastor in leading the congregation through tumultuous times, when heretics are leading some astray and others are suffering martyrdom. Through all these events the high calling of the pastoral office is there to lead the people.

Pastoral Ministry: Sound Teaching and Blameless Conduct

When Irenaeus discusses pastoral ministry, he continually cycles back to two essential characteristics: sound teaching and blameless conduct. The pastor, he argues, must be skilled in the art of theological reflection and experienced in living a holy life. When these two things are coordinated in the life of the pastor, there one finds a pastor who is in the line of the apostles. In one place, Irenaeus coordinates these three points in unity saying that faithful Christian leaders are those who "guard the doctrine of the apostles and who together with those of the priestly rank offer sound doctrine and blameless conduct for the formation and correction of the rest."[1] To hold the doctrine of the apostles, or to be in the line of the order of the priesthood, entails that a pastor will hold to sound teaching and blameless conduct. There

---

1. *Haer* 4.26.4.

are some who serve in the church who are heretics, like wolves in sheep's clothing who reveal themselves to hold to neither sound teaching nor blameless conduct and, as a result, prove that they are not in the line of the apostolic faith. In this chapter I discuss each of these points in turn, explaining what Irenaeus means by sound teaching, blameless conduct, and apostolic succession.

Sound Teaching

The role of the pastor is to offer up sound teaching of the Word of God. This entails two key practices: teaching according to the rule of faith, and discerning truth and error. First, the rule of faith, as I discussed in chapter two, is a summary of the teaching of the apostles, encapsulating in a few words what it is that the apostles believe. Sound teaching necessitates that the pastor teaches in accordance with the rule of faith, not adding to, nor subtracting from, the doctrine that was handed down. To aim is to guide Christians in incremental ways, through the Spirit, toward conformity to Christ's likeness. Sound teaching directs the people to the true knowledge of the doctrine of the apostles, which is also "a correct and harmonious explanation according to the Scriptures, without danger and without blasphemy."[2] For a pastor to impart sound teaching does not mean that every pastor agrees on every minute detail of doctrine and practice. Irenaeus gives examples where the presbyters disagree about the interpretation of Scripture, even though they all agree on the same fundamental points of doctrine. In other words, the rule of faith is the primary first principle, but within the bounds of the rule there are principled disagreements.

Irenaeus' discussion of the interpretation of the divine command in the Garden of Eden—to eat freely from any tree except the tree of knowledge of good and evil—provides a good example of the way that the rule of faith allows for diverse

---

2.   *Haer* 4.33.8

interpretations within the bounds of a unified confession.[3] The Lord said in Genesis 2:17 that the day they ate from the tree they would die, but in the narrative, it does not appear that they die immediately. The Gnostics use this passage to prove that God is a liar. The Lord in Genesis, in their view, is a lower depraved being, disconnected from the Gnostic heavenly realm. But Irenaeus argues that the only way to make sense of this passage, given the church's rule of faith, is to read it in accordance with the doctrine of God and interpret the passage in a way that demonstrates God is true and the serpent is a liar.[4] But even within the church there is no specific agreement about the proper way to make sense of the passage; instead, there are several legitimate ways of reading the passages that all prove God is true and the serpent is a liar. Some, for example, interpret the "day" in relationship with 2 Peter 3:8 (Psalm 90:4)—in Irenaeus' translation, "a day of the Lord is as a thousand years"—arguing that Adam died before he reaches that span of time. Others argue for a reading that takes death in a metaphorical sense, so that the day they ate, they were handed over to the power of death. Others connect the passage to Gensis 1:5, the first day of creation, and interpret it in a cosmic sense as one universal day of the Lord's reign, so they died within God's cosmic rule. Irenaeus assumes that even when they disagree, the presbyter will offer up the right reading of Scripture, finding Christ in the Scriptures like a treasure hidden in a field.[5] The right reading of Scripture will guide those who are faithful toward the teaching of the apostles.

In another place, Irenaeus shows disagreement over the dating of Easter, also known as the Quartodeciman controversary. This is one of the earliest known controversaries in the church outside the New Testament. The diversity of opinion regards not only the dating but the fasting associated with the holiday.

3. *Haer* 5.23.1–2.

4. *Haer* 5.23.1–2.

5. *Haer* 4.26.1.

Some, Irenaeus writes, "consider themselves bound to fast one day, others two days, others still more, while others [do so during] forty: the diurnal and the nocturnal hours they measure out together as their [fasting] day."[6] Irenaeus references a council between Polycarp, the bishop of Smyrna, and Anicetus, the bishop of Rome, concerning these issues. "And when the blessed Polycarp was sojourning in Rome in the time of Anicetus," Irenaeus writes, "although a slight controversy had arisen among them as to certain other points, they were at once well inclined towards each other [with regard to the matter in hand], not willing that any quarrel should arise between them upon this head."[7] Neither could persuade the other about their understanding of the practice. But nevertheless, "they parted in peace one from the other, maintaining peace with the whole Church, both those who did observe [this custom] and those who did not."[8] Despite these disagreements, Irenaeus argues, all of them "lived in peace one with another, and we also keep peace together."[9] Thus, in fact, the difference [in observing] the fast establishes the harmony of [our common] faith."[10] For Irenaeus, the unity in the differences is the point. The fact that they remain committed to the same faith and the same moral commitments demonstrates their immense unity of faith even with the apparent diversity.

Second, besides communicating the teaching of the church, "sound teaching" also implies that the pastor discerns truth from error. Irenaeus argues that is it important for those who know the teaching of the church, "to hold in suspicion the rest

---

6. Fragment 3. The translations of the fragments of Irenaeus' writings are taken from: "Fragments From the Lost Writings of Irenaeus," *The Ante-Nicene Fathers, Volume 1: The Apostolic Fathers, Justin Martyr,* Irenaeus, edited by Alexander Roberts and James Donaldson (Edinburgh: Christian Literature Publishing Company, 1885; reprint, New York: Scribners, 1899).

7. Fragment 3.

8. Fragment 3.

9. Fragment 3.

10. Fragment 3.

who depart from the original succession and assemble in any manner whatever."[11] These are leaders that show themselves to be "heretics, and evil-minded, or schismatics and puffed up and pleasing themselves, or again as hypocrites, acting for the sake of gain, or out of vainglory."[12] All of these have fallen away from the truth, Irenaeus reports. The pastors need to adjudicate the theological issues facing their congregation and be on guard against those who turn and who are actively trying to deceive them. Irenaeus uses the image of Nadab and Abihu offering up strange fire before the Lord to illustrate that, for those who bring foreign doctrines into the church, the Lord rejects their offering.[13]

The pastor also needs to help preserve the people of God from error, directing them back to the truth of the Scriptures. The heretics are like "slippery serpents" trying to escape at all points.[14] But the pastor should be there striving to turn them back to the truth. "If it is not easy for anyone to make a soul that is held captive by error to repent, still it is not altogether impossible for error to flee when it is brought face to face with the truth," Irenaeus writes.[15] The problem is that already there are some in the church who are even presbyters, that are "slaves to their own lusts and do not put the fear of God in first place in their hearts."[16] Irenaeus does not mince words about these leaders. They "heap contumely on others and are puffed up with the pride of priority seating, and do evil things in secret."[17] They believe that no one sees their deeds and live without any fear of God. Irenaeus implores his readers to "keep away from all such

11.   *Haer* 4.26.2.

12.   *Haer* 4.26.2.

13.   Lev. 10:1.

14.   *Haer* 3.2.3.

15.   *Haer* 3.2.3.

16.   *Haer* 4.26.3.

17.   *Haer* 4.26.3.

presbyters," and follow those who hold to the teaching of the apostles.[18] Some have already left the church, enticed by pride or heretical teaching. They previously "forsake the preaching of the Church accuse the holy presbyters with lack of intelligence."[19] But, Irenaeus continues, "they do not consider how much more valuable an unlettered pious person is than a blasphemous and bold sophist."[20] They reject the true teaching of the apostles and maintain lives that do not comport with Scripture. These heretics imagine that they have discovered some truth that lies beyond the scope of God, but in reality they are "like blind men who are led about by the blind led by the blind."[21] As a result, they show themselves to be outside the tradition of the church.

But in the true church there is the true teaching of the Scriptures and those who are walking in accordance with its teaching. Irenaeus entreats his readers, and all people, to "take refuge in the Church and be reared in her bosom and nourished by the Lord's Scriptures."[22] In the church, the people of God enjoy a regular feast of the Word of God, served up by their pastor, and enjoy its blessings. "Really, the Church, as a garden, is planted in this world," Irenaeus continues, and just as God implored Adam to eat from any tree of the garden, so does the Spirit of God encourage the faithful to "eat from every Scripture of the Lord," but do not eat "with a haughty mind."[23]

Blameless Conduct

Second, pastors need to maintain not only sound teaching, but also blameless conduct. Irenaeus calls the church to be blameless, or above reproach, in their spiritual lives. He indicates that not

18. *Haer* 4.36.4.
19. *Haer* 5.20.1.
20. *Haer* 5.20.1.
21. *Haer* 5.20.2.
22. *Haer* 5.20.2.
23. *Haer* 5.20.2.

all presbyters are living up to the standards that he envisions, so he encourages his readers to follow only those presbyters who remain faithful to the apostolic teaching. There are some presbyters who do not maintain sound teaching. Presbyters who "serve their own lusts, and, do not place the fear of God supreme in their hearts."[24] Rejecting the fear of God, these pastors have wandered away from the apostolic teaching and lack the virtue that the pastoral ministry demands. Instead, they are "puffed up with the pride of holding the chief seat, and work evil deeds in secret, saying, 'No man sees us.'"[25] These presbyters believe that their deeds will go unnoticed, that they can sin in secret without consequence. Irenaeus assures readers that the Lord will deal with these people; God sees their hearts.

One example Irenaeus mentions includes Tatian, a Christian convert under the tutelage of Justin Martyr.[26] Justin was an apologist in second-century Rome, who dabbled in various philosophical schools before converting to Christianity. Little is known about Tatian's background, but according to Irenaeus he studied with Justin. Irenaeus laments that some have fallen away from the church such as Tatian, who was "a follower of Justin" and, when he was under Justin's supervision, Tatian did not express any heretical views. Tatian is known for several works that supported the Christian faith, including his *Address to the Greeks*, which condemned pagan philosophy, and *Diatessaron*, which was a harmony of the four Gospels, synthesizing them into a combined narrative. But after Justin was martyred, Irenaeus reports that Tatian became prideful, desiring to be

---

24.   *Haer* 4.26.3.

25.   *Haer* 4.26.3.

26.   For more about Justin Martyr see, L. W. Barnard, *Justin Martyr: His Life and Thought* (Cambridge: Cambridge University Press, 2008). For more about Tatian see: Tatian, *Oratio ad Graecos and Fragments*, edited by Molly Whittaker (Oxford: Clarendon Press, 1982).

his own teacher, so he left the church and "composed his own standard of teaching."[27]

Irenaeus also coordinates several passages from Scripture to show that God will judge the unfaithful leaders and that the Lord will send faithful pastors. Irenaeus cites the Lord's warning in Luke 12:42-48 that God will deal justly with the rebellious Christian leaders. As the Lord promises, "if that wicked servant says to himself, 'My master is delayed,' and beings to beat his men-servants and maid-servants and eats and drinks and gets drunk, the master of the servant will come on a day when he does not know and in an hour he does not expect, and will cut him off and make him share the lot of the unfaithful."[28] God also promises to preserve his people through these leaders and to guide them to the appointed end. And until he does, he desires that his people avoid these false leaders, precisely because they do not maintain good doctrine and practice and, as a result, do not follow in the tradition of the apostles.

The words of the Lord in Luke 12:42-48 offer another promise. "Who is the faithful and wise steward, who his master has set over his household, to give them their food at the proper time? Blessed is that servant who is master when he comes will find so doing."[29] Alongside Luke 12, Irenaeus brings along other passages that promise that the Lord will send pastors to his people who are faithful and who will guide them in truth. Passages such as Isaiah 60:17 that, in Irenaeus' version reads, "I will give peace to your taskmasters and to your overseers righteousness."[30] Finally, both are confirmed in Paul's words in 1 Corinthians 12:28, "God has appointed in the Church, first Apostles, second Prophets, third teachers."[31] These are the kinds

---

27. *Haer* 1.28.1.

28. *Haer* 4.26.3.

29. *Haer* 4.26.5.

30. *Haer* 4.26.5.

31. *Haer* 4.26.5.

of leaders that the church nourishes. These promises indicate that the Lord will preserve the church through faithful ministers who maintain sound doctrine and lead blameless lives. These leaders will help direct the faithful down the straight and narrow path that leads to true life.

Irenaeus also provides several examples of faithful leadership drawn from key portions of the biblical witnesses, such as Moses, Samuel, and Paul. These leaders provide a way to envision the faithfulness of the pastor, the minister who stands before God and walks blamelessly. First, he turns to Moses, a leader who relied upon "a good conscience."[32] He points to Korah's Rebellion in Numbers 16 where Moses "justified himself before God," saying, "I have not taken anything of theirs out of covetousness; and I have not harmed one of them."[33] The rebellion against Moses claimed that he was prideful and desired to exalt himself above the assembly. Moses goes before the Lord and pleads his case, and the ground swallowed those who rebelled. Second, in Samuel's farewell address, he claims a clear conscience and confesses his blamelessness. He calls the people to witness, "I have lived with you from my youth until this day. Testify against me before the Lord and before his anointed, if I have taken any of your ox or ass, if I have domineered over anyone, or oppressed anyone, or if I have taken a bribe at anyone's hand or sandals."[34] "Testify against me," Samuel continues, "and I will restore it to you."[35] The people respond to Samuel and say, "You have not domineered over any of us, or oppressed us, or taken anything from any man's hand."[36] Finally, Irenaeus also turns to two examples from Paul's letters. Paul argues that he is not like others who are "adulterating God's word" through their actions, but he

---

32. *Haer* 4.26.4.

33. *Haer* 4.26.4. Num. 16:15 (Not ESV).

34. *Haer* 4.26.4.

35. *Haer* 4.26.4.

36. *Haer* 4.26.4. 1 Sam. 12:2–5 (Not ESV).

rather speaks out of sincerity as one sent from God, saying, "We have wronged no one, we have corrupted no one, we have taken advantage of no one."[37] These virtues express the kind of leader that the people of God are called to follow: the blameless teacher who is able to provide sound teaching and who lives the spiritual life in faith. These leaders are not always perfect examples of godliness, but in moments like these the community of faith can discern models of faithfulness for them to follow.

Apostolic Succession

Irenaeus is one of the earliest defenders of the succession of bishops in the church. But even at this early stage there is a struggle to maintain the unity of this succession. Even in the second century, identifying with the Christian community is not merely a matter of identifying with an ecclesial body that has some link to the apostles, but of aligning with a body that does in fact hold to the apostolic confession and is committed to maintaining a holy life. Some within the church are among those who will remain faithful, which is why Irenaeus holds together apostolic succession with "sound teaching" and "blameless conduct." These are the qualifications that assure one that they are in the same line as the apostles. Irenaeus stresses the importance of the church at Rome because of the apostles, Peter and Paul, who helped found the church there. Given that both apostles have connections to that church, Irenaeus argues that the faith taught by these apostles comes down through a succession of bishops, who all preserve the faith. Irenaeus provides a list of names, called a succession list, of the bishop of Rome, arguing that the unity of teaching is "the fullest proof that it is one and the same life-giving faith that has been preserved in the Church from the apostles until now, and had been handed down in truth."[38]

---

37. *Haer* 4.26.4. 2 Cor. 7:2; 2 Cor. 2:17.
38. *Haer* 3.3.3.

Besides Peter and Paul, Irenaeus knows Polycarp, who was appointed bishop of Smyrna and who had conversations with the Apostle John and "always taught the things that he has learned from the apostles, which he also handed on to the Church and which alone are true."[39] He also mentions that "the Church at Ephesus, which was founded by Paul but in which John remained till the time of Trajan, is also a true witness of the tradition of the apostles."[40] All of these churches preserve the same faith and the same teaching. Irenaeus argues that the church offers a "distinctive character of the Body of Christ according to the succession of the Bishops, to whom they [apostles] handed down to the Church, which is in every place."[41] Irenaeus claims that even his community has received the knowledge of the doctrine of the apostles, which he explains in several ways saying that this knowledge is a "safeguarding without fictional matter, the fullest account of the Scriptures, with neither addition nor subtraction," and a reading the Scriptures "without falsification; and "a correct and harmonious explanation according to the Scriptures, without danger and without blasphemy."[42] Only those who maintain the true faith and live blamelessly can find their continuity with the apostles. Anyone who wishes "to see the truth can view in the whole Church the tradition of the apostles that has been manifested in the whole world" and can look to the church where there are bishops and a succession of men who lead the church. [43] The apostles desired that those who succeed them "should be very perfect and blameless in every respect."[44]

---

39.   *Haer* 3.3.4.
40.   *Haer* 3.3.4.
41.   *Haer* 4.33.8.
42.   *Haer* 4.33.8.
43.   *Haer* 3.3.1.
44.   *Haer* 3.3.1.

The fact that Irenaeus is making this claim, however, is because there are divisions and struggles to maintain the same faith. From our vantage point, we know that adhering to "sound teaching" and "blameless conduct" will be even more challenging as the church continues to expand and grow. But even in the earliest centuries of the church, there is a struggle to maintain faithfulness amid those who deviate from the gospel by either teaching error or succumbing to immorality.

Pastoral Ministry: Baptism and Eucharist

The pastoral calling to adhere to sound teaching and blameless conduct helps frame the importance of baptism and the Eucharist. Irenaeus recognizes the importance of liturgy for spiritual formation. In one place, reflecting upon the Eucharist, he argues that "our doctrine is in harmony with the Eucharist, and the Eucharist in turn confirms our doctrine."[45] This logical summary is reminiscent of the premise "what is prayed is what is believed" (lex orandi, lex credenda). This is an often-repeated maxim throughout church history, which means that believers are often formed through the regular habits of worship and liturgy. His view of the Eucharist is in accordance with what has been taught, and what has been taught is shaped by his view of the Eucharist. This shows that even in the early years of the church, the liturgy of the church is guiding the faithful. The sound teaching is imparted to new converts as they prepare for baptism, while, at the same time, the worship reinforces the doctrines that are taught. These two sacraments, baptism and the Eucharist, work together to disciple the people and lead them in sanctification.

Baptism

Beginning with his view of baptism, this practice signals one's entrance into the community. In baptism they confess the faith

---

45. Haer 4.18.5.

that was delivered from the apostles, celebrate the reception of the Spirit, and welcome new members into the congregation. Baptism is the culmination of a longer period of discipleship. Irenaeus would not permit someone to join the church or go into the baptismal waters who did not understand the basic contours of the faith. New converts living in a pagan world need to know what the Christian faith teaches and how they are to live in light of it. Irenaeus does not give a specific timeframe for catechesis, but there is no question that he imagines the process as an extended program. New converts need to understand the gospel and the vision of life that the Bible is calling them to. Irenaeus wants his followers to remember this baptism and look to their baptism as an important moment that involved their confession of the faith and entrance into the community.

Summarizing his view of baptism, Irenaeus writes, "we have received baptism for the remission of sins, in the name of God the Father, and in the name of Jesus Christ, the Son of God, [who was] incarnate, and died, and was raised, and in the Holy Spirit of God." For Irenaeus, baptism "is the seal of eternal life, and rebirth unto God, that we may no longer be the sons of mortal men, but of the eternal and everlasting God."[46] The key elements are here: the triune name, the imagery of new birth and redemption, the allusion of the sealing of the Spirit and the promise of resurrection, and a change in identity from a son of man to a son of God. Each of these elements helps establish the way that baptism provided a theologically rich transition point for people.

First, Irenaeus observes that baptism should proceed under the name of the Father, Son, and Spirit, thus stressing the importance of confession and the trinitarian act of redemption involved in baptism. Irenaeus alludes to Matthew 28:19 and describes how baptism marks the transition into the people of God. "And for this reason," Irenaeus writes, "the baptism of our

---

46. *Epid* 3.

regeneration takes place through these three articles, granting us regeneration unto God the Father through His Son by the Holy Spirit: for those who bear the Spirit of God are led to the Word, that is to the Son, while the Son presents [them] to the Father, and the Father furnishes incorruptibility."[47] Baptism also marks the indwelling of the Spirit and membership into the people of God. All of these points means that baptism signifies the entrance into the community, and that it is the "seal of eternal life" and "new birth unto God."[48] Those who receive baptism are no longer "sons of mortal men, but of the eternal and perpetual God," pointing to a transition into a new community and new self-understanding.[49] The community is on a journey together along the path of redemption.

Eucharist
Turning to the Eucharist, Irenaeus stresses several points. The Eucharist is a sacrifice or perpetual offering to God. It involves a spiritual presence with both material and spiritual realities in the elements, and it functions to nourish Christians, preparing them to grow in godliness as they await resurrection. First, a key theme about the Eucharist is sacrifice. Against his Gnostic opponents, Irenaeus wants to emphasize the unity between the Old and New Testaments. In the case of the Eucharist, he links it with the sacrificial system of the Old Testament arguing that this offering could never appease sin. Instead, the Eucharist represents the fulfillment of sacrifices. Summarizing his view, Irenaeus writes, "sacrifices do not sanctify man, for God does not need sacrifices; but the intention, when pure, of the one who offers, sanctifies the sacrifice and assures that God will accept it

---

47. *Epid* 7.
48. *Epid* 7.
49. *Epid* 7.

as from a friend."[50] The church, then, "offers with simplicity, rightly as her give been regarded by God as a pure sacrifice."[51]

Second, Irenaeus sees in the elements a spiritual presence. In the elements there is the "communion and union of the flesh and Spirit" that is of both the earthly and spiritual realities.[52] Explaining his view, Irenaeus writes, "just as the bread, which is from the earth, when it receives the invocation of God, is no longer common bread, but the Eucharist, consisting of two things, the earthly and the heavenly."[53] These two realities, moreover, feed the body and prepare the body for life with God, so that when people receive the Eucharist they "are no longer perishable, since they possess the hope of the resurrection."[54] The two realities are present: the material, bread and wine, and the Spirit. Together both elements nourish the body and provide growth in godliness that awaits resurrection in the kingdom to come.

Irenaeus also sees in the Eucharist an important defense against a Gnostic anthropology. Some Gnostic groups host perversions of the Eucharist rite which use the bread and wine but apply them to different realities.[55] For the Christian, the Eucharist represents the salvation of both the body and the soul. If the body is not saved, "then neither did the Lord redeem us with his blood, nor is the cup of the Eucharist a communion in his blood, nor is the bread we break a communion in his body."[56] For blood can only come from veins and flesh, and whatsoever else makes up the substance of man, just as the Word of God was actually made. His own blood has redeemed us. As

---

50. *Haer* 4.18.3.

51. *Haer* 4.18.4.

52. *Haer* 4.18.5.

53. *Haer* 4.18.5.

54. *Haer* 4.18.5.

55. *Haer* 1.13.2.

56. *Haer* 5.2.2.

the apostle writes, through Christ "we have redemption through His blood, even the remission of sins."[57]

Third, the Eucharist serves to strengthen the lives of the Christians and prepares them for the Lord's work in the world and for his resurrection. Responding to his Gnostic opponents again, Irenaeus writes, "we are his members, we are also nourished by the creation."[58] The same God who created the world has given us created things to nourish us and fit us for growth. So, the cup is "from the creation in his Blood, from which he gives growth to our blood; and he affirmed that the bread which is from the creation in his Body, from which he gives growth to our bodies."[59] Through the Eucharist the Christian is nourished, body and soul, and is fitted for the resurrection. Before this doctrine all the arguments of the heretics crumble, since the Lord "redeemed us by his blood, and gave his soul for our souls and his flesh for our flesh, and poured out the Father's Spirit to effect the union and communion of God with man."[60] God did this by "bringing down God to men through the Spirit, and by bringing man up to God through the incarnation."[61]

To illustrate how the Eucharist nourishes the faithful and prepares them for resurrection, he turns to the image of a vine tree and a stock of wheat. Just as "a branch of the vine, when placed in the ground, will produce fruit in due time, and the grain of wheat that falls into the ground and decomposes rises multiplied, through God's Spirit who holds all things together."[62] From the produce of the vine and the wheat come wine and bread, which grow thanks to the wisdom of God who has fashioned the creation to allow for this kind of growth. From

---

57. *Haer* 5.2.2.

58. *Haer* 5.2.2.

59. *Haer* 5.2.2.

60. *Haer* 5.1.1.

61. *Haer* 5.1.1.

62. *Haer* 5.2.3.

this produce, humanity is nourished through the Eucharist, and though the bodies of the faithful are buried in the earth, and decompose into the earth, they will rise in due time when the Word of God bestows resurrection on them for the glory of God the Father."[63] In this way, both the bread and the wine nourish the Christian, preparing them for the life of the world to come.

Prayer

Alongside his vision of the sacraments, Irenaeus believes prayer is essential to the spiritual life, serving as a steady reminder of the work of God in their lives and patiently orienting their thinking toward the one true God. Irenaeus often speaks of prayer in his writings, typically in terms of praying for others, thereby demonstrating a life of prayer. In several other places Irenaeus pauses to pray, most often for his enemies, thus modeling prayer for his readers. First, Irenaeus points to Christ as the model for prayer. When Christ suffered, he prayed. Though his captors abused and mistreated him even to the point of death on the cross, Christ, in his "long-suffering, patience, compassion, and goodness," still prayed "Father, forgive them, for they know not what they do."[64] He had already proclaimed to his followers, "love your enemies and pray for those who hate you," and Christ did this on the cross when he prayed "even for those who put him to death."[65] Irenaeus also looks to Christ as an example of fortitude in prayer and others who follow his example, always praying for those who are lost in the delusions of false doctrines. For when Christ "was reviled, [he] did not revile in return, and when he suffered, he did not threaten, and when he endured tyranny, He asked the Father to forgive them who had crucified Him."[66] In his moment of greatest persecution, Christ prayed

---

63. Haer 5.2.3.
64. Haer 3.18.5.
65. Haer 3.18.5.
66. Haer 3.16.9.

for his enemies, and Irenaeus implores the faithful to follow this example. Stephen, too, whom Irenaeus terms the "Teacher of martyrdom," prayed for those who killed him, saying, "Lord do not hold this sin against them."[67]

Irenaeus attempts to follow Christ's example. There are several places in his writings where Irenaeus pauses to pray for others, both believers and heretics. A simple example of prayer is the way Irenaeus begins his *Demonstration* with his prayer for his friend: "Knowing, my dear Marcianus, your zeal for godliness, which alone brings man to eternal life, I congratulate you and pray that, preserving your faith intact, you may be pleasing to God, your Creator."[68] In another prayer for his readers, Irenaeus prays that the readers of his work might come to believe and to confess faith in God. He begins with an extended invocation, praising the one who created all things: "I too call upon You, O Lod, God of Abraham, and God of Isaac and God of Jacob and Israel, who are the Father of our Lord Jesus Christ, the God who because of the multitude of Your mercies has shown Your good pleasure toward us that we might know You; who made heaven and earth, who has dominion over all things; who are the only true God, above whom there is no other God."[69] Then he prays for his readers, through Christ and the Spirit, that God may "grant that everyone who reads this writing may know You, that You alone are God, and may be strengthened in You, and may separate himself from every heretical, godless, and impious doctrine."[70]

Through these prayers, Irenaeus demonstrates pastoral piety— the love for those within the church and a longing for a pure church. The prayers are Trinitarian and layered with the threads of his theological vision of the spiritual life. In these prayers we

---

67.   *Haer* 3.12.13.

68.   *Epid* 1.

69.   *Haer* 3.6.4.

70.   *Haer* 3.6.4.

can see the intersection between the doctrine of God and the practical responsibilities of pastoring. Irenaeus longs to see the church flourish and his readers grow in their love for God.

Second, in other places he explicitly prays for his opponents. As he closes his third book of *Against Heresies,* Irenaeus pauses to pray for Gnostics. "We do indeed pray that these men may not remain in the pit which they themselves have dug," Irenaeus prays, "that Christ may be formed in them, and that they may know the Framer and Maker of this universe, the only true God and Lord of all."[71] In another place, Irenaeus prays for the Gnostics, that they might not remain in the ignorance of their belief, but turn to trust the one true God. In a prayer like this, Irenaeus imitates Christ's praying for his enemies. He prays that the heretics might not continue to wallow in their error and erroneous doctrines writing, "We, however, pray that these men do not remain in the ditch they have dug, but will separate themselves from such a Mother, forsake the Profundity, depart from the void, and abandon the shadow."[72] He also prays that they might be "converted to God's church," and that "they may be born legitimately and Christ may be formed in them; and that they may know the Maker and Creator of this universe, the only true God and the Lord of all things."[73] He prays these things out of his own love for his opponents, writing, "We petition these things for them, loving them more than they think they love themselves. For our love, since it is true, is salvific for them—if only they will accept it. It is like a bitter medicine that removes the foreign and useless flesh around the wound, for it deflates their pride and haughtiness."[74] He concludes by promising that he will never grow weary of trying with all his strength to see them come to faith in Christ. His final words communicate the

---

71. *Haer* 3.25.7.

72. *Haer* 3.25.7.

73. *Haer* 3.25.7.

74. *Haer* 3.25.7.

kind of fortitude that should mark the Christian life. Irenaeus will never grow weary of trying to persuade his opponents, trying to reach out to them and help guide them to faith in Christ. Adding to this prayer Irenaeus writes, "Perhaps, by convincing some of these by means of the very doctrine of Christ, I can persuade them to give up this sort of error and desist from the blasphemy against their Maker, who alone is God and the Father of our Lord Jesus Christ, Amen."[75]

These prayers demonstrate the importance of the authentic spiritual life even in the middle of controversies and persecution. The regular appearance of these prayers in Irenaeus' writing evidence a regular habit of prayer in his life. Irenaeus recognizes that prayer orients the heart, guiding the people of God toward the good life found in Christ. In many ways, Irenaeus models prayer for his readers, reminding them that personal piety and prayer are essential to the spiritual life.

Martyrdom

Finally, for Irenaeus there is a special place for martyrs who have paid the ultimate sacrifice for the cause of Christ. He specifically emphasizes the way martyrs despise death, and provides several examples of faithful martyrs as he calls the church to emulate those who are faithful to the end. First, in the ancient world, the church lived in a culture that did not share its theological or moral convictions. There was a posture of skepticism if not outright ridicule, for Christian beliefs and practices. For Irenaeus and his community, this meant living with the abiding posture of suffering. The church, Irenaeus remarks, "because of her love for God, sends a multitude of martyrs ahead to the Father everywhere and always."[76] The heretics, on the other hand, do not share the same level of faithfulness, and some even claim that "it is not even necessary to have such martyrdom (witness),

---

75. *Haer* 3.25.7.
76. *Haer* 4.33.9.

because their doctrine is the true martyrdom (witness)."[77] They do not have martyrs willing to suffer and die for their convictions. Only the church upholds "intact the opprobrium of those who suffer persecution for the sake of justice, and who endure all the pains and are put to death on account of love for God and on account of the confession of his Son."[78] Irenaeus even uses the vivid image of amputation to describe martyrdom. While the church is always having "members amputate, but soon increases her members and becomes whole again."[79] Moreover, these sufferings and martyrdoms, initially weaken the church, but eventually these acts only serve to strengthen her and increase membership. As he indicates to his community, this may take on many forms—even possibly giving one's life—but through suffering and death there is life and strength. The martyrs, Irenaeus writes, "despise death, not after the infirmity of the flesh, but because of the readiness of the Spirit."[80] They are not like the Gnostics who despise death because they reject the material world, quite the opposite. They despise death because, through the strength of the Spirit, they know they will rise again. For the Spirit "absorbs the weakness [of the flesh], it possesses the flesh as an inheritance in itself, and from both of these is formed a living man, — living, indeed, because he partakes of the Spirit, but man, because of the substance of flesh."[81]

Irenaeus calls the faithful to imitate Christ and look to the other examples of suffering and martyrdom in the lives of the patriarchs, prophets, and apostles. On one occasion, he points to the Lord's words in Matthew 10:28, "Fear not them which kill the body, but are not able to kill the soul; but rather fear

---

77. *Haer* 4.33.9.

78. *Haer* 4.33.9.

79. *Haer* 4.33.9.

80. *Haer* 5.9.2.

81. *Haer* 5.9.2.

Him who is able to send both soul and body into hell."[82] He acknowledges that this passage indicates that there will be "both those who should suffer persecution" and "those who should have to be scourged and slain because of Him."[83] But in the moment of suffering and trial, the faithful should not deny the Lord, nor lose heart. Irenaeus speaks of some who "proceeded to such a degree of temerity, that they even pour contempt upon the martyrs, and vituperate those who are slain on account of the confession of the Lord."[84] For those tempted by this kind of denial, he warns them that they ought to rightly fear the Lord, who will be their ultimate judge and who "is able to send both soul and body into hell."[85] Instead, the faithful ought to look to the example of Christ who, while suffering on the cross, exclaimed, "Father, forgive them, for they know not what they do."[86] In this act, "the longsuffering, patience, compassion, and goodness of Christ are exhibited."[87]

Others in Scripture mirror Christ's example. Many in the church endured persecution "like the ancient Prophets, as the Lord said, For so they persecuted the prophets before you."[88] The prophets, Irenaeus argues, foretold that many would "suffer persecution and be stoned and killed."[89] Jacob, for example, received the blessing from Esau and as a result suffered "the ploys and persecutions" of his brother in the same way that the church suffers from the Jews.[90] David too suffered "persecution from Saul on account of justice, and fled from King Saul and did

---

82.   *Haer* 3.18.5.
83.   *Haer* 3.18.5.
84.   *Haer* 3.18.5.
85.   *Haer* 3.18.5.
86.   *Luke* 23:34.
87.   *Haer* 3.18.5.
88.   *Haer* 4.33.9.
89.   *Haer* 4.33.10.
90.   *Haer* 4.21.3.

not take revenge on his enemy."[91] Though David and others did not always live in ways that were pleasing to God, nevertheless they did suffer for the sake of their faith in God. Irenaeus also cites the words of the Lord that predict the church's suffering. The apostles and their disciples, Irenaeus writes, were "called to perfection" implying a call to pursue Christ even in suffering.[92] Irenaeus reminds his readers what Christ used to say to the disciples: "And you will be brought before governors and kings for my sake... and some of you they will scourge and put to death and persecute you from town to town."[93] His disciples would suffer and follow the Lord in his passion.

Among these, Irenaeus discusses Stephen and Polycarp (not to mention the martyrs of Lyons and Vienne discussed in the opening chapter of this book).[94] When he speaks of Stephen, Irenaeus observes that he was "chosen by the apostles as the first deacon, and who was the first of all men to follow in the footsteps of the Lord's martyrdom, having been the first who was put to death for professing Christ, spoke courageously to the people and taught them."[95] Stephen made a bold confession and was slain for confessing Christ and instructing the people in the faith. Similarly, Polycarp, the early Christian bishop of Smyrna, when he was "a very old man, having most gloriously and most nobly suffering martyrdom."[96] Alongside Christ and the prophets, these and others are held out as the examples to model.

But not everyone was faithful to the end. In the introduction, I describe the letter detailing the martyrdom in Irenaeus' community, and mention that some ten people capitulated to

---

91.   *Haer* 4.27.1

92.   *Haer* 3.12.13. Heb. 2:10; 7:28; 8:1.

93.   *Haer* 3.18.5.

94.   *Haer* 3.3.3. In his list of bishops of Rome, Irenaeus mentions "Telephorus, who was gloriously martyred."

95.   *Haer* 3.12.10.

96.   *Haer* 3.3.3–4.

the demands to worship idols. These ten Christians "caused great pain and immeasurable sorrow for us, and undercut the desire of the rest who had not been arrested."[97] The rest of the church was concerned that others might follow their example and capitulate. They were more terrified that someone should deny Christ and worship idols than they were at the thought of suffering. The letter describes how the people of faith "were greatly distraught on account of the lack of clarity of [their] confession, not dreading the punishments that were impending, but fearing that someone might fall away while we looked forward to the end."[98] Amid the suffering of his community and elsewhere, Irenaeus implores Christians to look to Christ and to the example of faithful, steadfast Christians who remained faithful even unto death.

Conclusion

Contained within Irenaeus' theological writings are many discussions and descriptions of pastoral theology. Irenaeus is concerned over who is leading the church. Above all things the two qualities of a good pastor are sound teaching and blameless conduct. The pastor should be skilled in the art of distinguishing truth and error, and he should be an exemplar in virtue. These two features are sure signs of apostolic succession, or that the presbyter is found within the tradition of the apostolic teaching. The sacraments of baptism and the Lord's Supper are central to the church's ministry, helping their people mature in the faith and guiding them toward a great love for God and neighbor. His examples of prayers perform a similar function. He regularly demonstrates the importance of prayer, praying for the church and for his enemies. Finally, in Irenaeus' day, suffering and martyrdom were abiding concerns. Irenaeus is aware of the challenge to remain faithful, and he celebrates those who have

---

97. Eusebius, *History of the Church*, 5.1.11.

98. Eusebius, *History of the Church*, 5.1.12.

given their lives for the cause of Christ. Irenaeus views all these features of ministry as essential for the life of the church in the ancient world. In the next chapter, I explain Irenaeus' vision of the spiritual life that challenges the way people of faith live.

4

THE SPIRITUAL LIFE

Irenaeus had many formidable opponents, and the rule of faith received at baptism intended to help navigate those communities. His struggles with the Gnostics, philosophers, and Jews were not just a matter of competing ways of reading, but completely different views of reality. The rule of faith summarized the way that Irenaeus viewed all things, helping to guide a proper theological method with the right ordering of knowledge. The calling of the pastor was to lead people in this vision of God, showing them the Christian way of life. Christians inhabit a world where God reigns and calls his people to a holy life.

Now in this chapter, I want to look at Irenaeus' understanding of the spiritual life. I begin with his understanding of the human person. The natural human being comprises body and soul but remains immature without the indwelling of the Spirit who leads both body and soul toward incorruption. Next, I discuss the concepts of the image and likeness of God, which help frame the beginning and end of the spiritual life. The whole human person, created body and soul in the image of God, is conformed to the likeness of God, fitted and prepared to behold the glory of God. Finally, I discuss recapitulation and resurrection, which offer two key structural beams in Irenaeus' scheme. Both help refute the Gnostic misconceptions of the human person.

The Economy and the Human Person

While Irenaeus' theological vision begins with God, he also situates the human person in God's economy and elevates the important work of God in creation. Irenaeus took great pains to defend the nature of a human person, not just because the Gnostics rejected the body as any meaningful part of human identity, but also because the origin, growth, and destiny of the human person is the work of God. Gnostic anthropology generally disparages the body as a prison for the divine spark that resides inside. This, Irenaeus argues, blasphemes God by denying salvation to the body. The whole material world and the human person is a creation of God; human beings in communion with God are the centerpiece of creation, growing incrementally in conformity to the divine likeness. In Irenaeus' summary, "God is the glory of humanity, but humanity is the vessel of God's working, of all His wisdom and power."[1] For Irenaeus, the body is an essential part of the human person because, according to the Scripture, humanity is created body and soul. At the same time humanity is also fitted with reason and freedom, which help the person mature.

Body, Soul, and Spirit

Irenaeus is clear that the human person is a work of God created body and soul. Irenaeus says it plainly: "Humanity is, however, a mixture of soul and flesh who has been formed according to God's likeness and fashioned by his hands, that is, by the Son and the Holy Spirit."[2] The "hands of God" is a Trinitarian analogy Irenaeus commonly uses and one that emphasizes the goodness

1. *Haer* 3.20.2.
2. *Haer* 4.pf.4.

of creation as the work of God.[3] While the rest of creation was "spoken" into existence, the formation of the human person involved a personal touch. "For by the Father's hands, namely, the Son and the Holy Spirit," Irenaeus writes, "man, and not part of man, is made to the image and the likeness of God."

Irenaeus recognizes, however, that a human person created body and soul is not, in and of itself, enough to inch toward perfection and grow in godliness. The person needs the Spirit of God who prepares and fits the person for beholding the glory of God. "Now, the soul and the 'Spirit' can be a part of man, but by no means the [whole] man," Irenaeus writes, "for the perfect man consists of the mingling and the union of the soul, which assumed the Father's 'Spirit,' and which has been united with the flesh, which was fashioned after the image of God."[4] The language of "perfect man" is an allusion to 1 Corinthians 2:6, "we speak wisdom among the perfect," and those who are "perfect" are persons who "have received God's Spirit."[5] The soul or the spirit without the body would merely be part of the person; it would be "man's spirit" or "God's Spirit" not a "spiritual man," to cite Irenaeus' distinction.[6] But when the Spirit of God is united with the soul and the body, "the man has become spiritual and perfect because of the outpouring of the Spirit."[7] Anyone who denies that salvation includes both soul and *body*, deny the goodness of the creator's work.

To explain the difference between body and soul, Irenaeus turns to Romans 8:11, "But if the Spirit of him who raised Jesus from the dead dwells in you, then he who raised Christ from the dead will give life to your mortal bodies."[8] Just as Christ

---

3. *Haer* 4.pf.4; 4.20.1; 5.6.1; 5.28.4.
4. *Haer* 5.6.1.
5. *Haer* 5.6.1.
6. *Haer* 5.6.1.
7. *Haer* 5.6.1.
8. *Haer* 5.7.1.

rose from the dead and showed the disciples the wounds on his body, so also will God raise up the mortal bodies of all people. But, Irenaeus asks, what are "mortal bodies"? Mortal bodies cannot be the breath of life that was given to all people. Genesis 2:7 described God breathing the breath of life into the nostrils of man and the man becoming a living soul; the breath is an incorporeal thing, not material like a body. And one cannot call the soul "mortal" since it is "the breath of life" that is given in creation and enables participation with God. Nor is the mortal body the Spirit that indwells the person, for the spirit is "not composed into parts, but simple, which cannot dissolve."[9] Thus, the mortal body is the flesh, the body that was formed from the earth and that will die in the dust, only to be raised again to new life. The mortal body is sown in the ground like a grain of wheat; it rots in the earth, until it springs forth in glorious resurrection. "What is more dishonorable than death flesh?" Irenaeus asks, alluding to 1 Corinthians 15:43. A body that had the breath of life now lays inanimate, decomposing and rotting. But, Irenaeus queries, what is more "honorable than the flesh that raises and receives imperishability?"[10] The body is sown in weakness and raised in power through the Spirit, becoming a "spiritual body."

Irenaeus also understands the relationship between the body, soul, and Spirit in a progressive sense. The breath of life is one thing, it is given to all people; the Spirit of God was given specifically from God, poured out through the New Covenant of adoption. The breath of life is breathed into the face of Adam, providing him a living soul. Irenaeus draws a distinction between the "breath of life" and the "life-giving spirit" who comes later. "For the breath of life, which makes a living soul is one thing, while the Spirit who gives like and makes man spiritual is something else," writes Irenaeus.[11] He observes this distinction

---

9.   Haer 5.7.1.

10. Haer 5.7.2.

11. Haer 5.12.2.

between breath and Spirit in Isaiah 57:16 which describes how the Lord created the heavens and earth and "gives breath to the people on it and spirit to those who walk on it."[12] The breath, therefore, is temporal, but the Spirit is eternal, meaning that the breath "is vigorous for a while and continues on for some time, then it departs, leaving that [body], in which it was, breathless."[13] But the Spirit "envelops men from within and without," leading people toward communion with God. In summary, the Word of God and the Spirit, together "having been united to the ancient substance of the handiwork of Adam, made man living and perfect, capable of receiving the perfect Father."[14]

The notions of growth and participation are key themes threading together Irenaeus' discussions of anthropology.[15] Irenaeus believes that Adam and Eve were without sin in the garden, but immature and not perfect. Perfection is the end of the road, the destiny for the believer. It involves a long process of growth and education which help the Christian navigate the rough terrains of life. Irenaeus uses the image of a sponge or fire to argue (against the Gnostics) that the body can partake of life and be fitted for resurrection. Just as a sponge soaks up water, and a torch possess fire, so can the body partake of life both now and in the age to come.[16] God has the power to confer life upon his creatures, and God has granted life to all people who possess the breath of life. He cites Paul's discussion in 1 Corinthians 15:45-46, writing, "But it is not first the spiritual that is first," Irenaeus writes, "but the physical is first, and then the spiritual."[17] Irenaeus has in mind here the Gnostics who argue that the spiritual person is one who possesses the

---

12. *Haer* 5.12.2.

13. *Haer* 5.12.2.

14. *Haer* 5.1.3. 1 Cor. 15:22.

15. Osborn, *Irenaeus of Lyons*, 230, 256.

16. *Haer* 3.3.3.

17. *Haer* 5.12.2.

divine spark residing within them. For his part, Irenaeus sees the formation of the person as the natural or animal person, followed by the spiritual person who comes later: "For it was necessary first that man be fashioned; next, that what was fashioned receive the soul; then, that it receive communion of the Spirit."[18] The order is important, signifying the movement toward perfection, through participation in the Spirit who guides the faithful toward communion with God.

Knowledge of Good and Evil

Second, not only is the human person created body and soul, but the soul is also endowed with properties of reason and freedom which enable the human person to grow in godliness through the Spirit. The breath is the soul, given to all people; it is temporal, increasing and continuing for a season, but then it departs in death, leaving its body destitute of breath and awaiting the resurrection. Irenaeus distinguishes between what we might call "animation," the conscience of the natural person, and "vivification," the empowering of the Holy Spirit.[19] These are different types of participation in God. The breath is given to all, while the Spirit is given only to the faithful.

The first sense, animation, refers to general consciences and reason; it is the capacity, despite sin, to discern right from wrong. In this sense, the breath of life is the soul, which is given to all people in Genesis and endows all people with reason.[20] This reason includes the mental powers to discern good from evil. It is a kind of natural law written on the hearts of all people that testifies to the reality and goodness of God. Irenaeus explains this reasoning in terms of a "twofold perception of knowledge": the knowledge of "the good of obedience" to God and "the evil

---

18. *Haer* 5.12.2.

19. Osborn, *Irenaeus of Lyons*, 224.

20. *Haer* 5.1.3.

of disobedience" toward God.[21] Just as the tongue experiences bitter and sweet, and sight can distinguish between black and white, so the mind, which experiences both good and evil, is able to discern that is it good to obey God.[22]

There is a pedagogical feature to evil and suffering that a person learns through the course of life. A human person is able, through experience or by discerning their morality and life, to learn good and evil. Humanity can be held accountable for their actions, for they have the knowledge of good and evil. In Irenaeus' logic, the difference between good and evil is the difference between life and death—between flourishing and deteriorating. Experience in this life imparts the knowledge that to disobey God takes life away from a person, and destroying life is evil. Believing in God, on the other hand, gives life, which is good.[23]

Irenaeus raises the question, "How can he be immortal who in his moral nature did not obey his Maker?"[24] Coming to believe in Christ is no easy transition, and Irenaeus knows this living in a pagan world and ministering to Celts and Gnostics. Salvation must be a work of God, who foreknows all things and who has already prepared "fit dwellings for both" those who seek the light and those who seek the darkness.[25] Only through "faith and subjection" to God will the human person "receive his [God's] art and will be God's perfect work."[26] In their freedom, humanity has the capacity to experience both good and evil, which provides wisdom for the spiritual life. How would the human person have "discernment of the good if he

21.   Haer 4.39.1.
22.   Haer 4.39.1.
23.   Haer 4.39.1.
24.   Haer 4.39.1.
25.   Haer 4.39.1.
26.   Haer 4.39.1.

was ignorant of its contrary?"[27] Irenaeus asks. When the human person experiences both good and evil they develop a "twofold perception," developing knowledge of both good and evil so that through discernment, people will choose "better things."[28] The better thing is ultimately life with God, both in the present age and in the age to come.

Image and Likeness

Building upon Irenaeus' basic anthropology are the specific theological concepts of the image and likeness of God, as well as the discussion of recapitulation and resurrection (mentioned in the next section). These are complex theological ideas that function like bridges, linking his vision of salvation history, and bringing together many of the anthropological points previously mentioned. The relationship between image and likeness in Irenaeus's works can be mystifying because he can appear to use the terms inconsistently. But when placed within the scope of salvation history, the terms help frame his vision for the human person.

On the one hand, the image and likeness of God are closely-related concepts, so he, at times, will speak about them in a unified, nearly synonymous way. The image of God and the likeness to God frame the nature of the human person and their relationship to God. On the other hand, he interprets them in different senses that relate to the growth of the human person toward resurrection and beatitude. Image and likeness help explain how the human person, who has lost the image and likeness, is slowly, through the work of Christ and the Spirit, recovering that which was lost and being assimilated to God.

Turning to the terms themselves, first, Irenaeus interprets the image of God in a couple ways. The image of God refers

---

27.   *Haer* 4.39.1.

28.   *Haer* 4.39.1.

to the "form and substance" of the human person.[29] More specifically, the image of God has a personal sense that is tied to the incarnate Christ. The incarnate Son is the archetypal image used to create Adam. "For in former times it was said that man was created after the image of God, but the image was not shown," Irenaeus writes, "for the Word, after whose image man had been created, was as yet invisible."[30] The image of God, that is the incarnate Son of God, was lost because the image was not visible. In the incarnation, humanity beheld the true image of God—the true form of humanity after whose image Adam was created. In Christ, the image and likeness that were lost in Adam were regained—or in Irenaeus' words, in the incarnation Christ furnished salvation for the people of God, so that "in Christ Jesus we might receive what we had lost in Adam, namely, to be according to the image and likeness of God."[31] In this sense, the terms are virtually synonymous, tied up in the person of Christ who, in his person, displays the image and likeness to God that were lost in Adam. Humanity, then, is slowly and methodically conformed to Christ, so that they too regain what was lost in Adam.

At the same time, Irenaeus also interprets the image of God in this sense of "reason" and "freedom." Both terms are attributes of the natural person, since all people are created in the image of God. In the beginning when Adam was made, "he was free and master of himself, having been made by God in this way, that he should rule over everything upon the earth."[32] In his freedom, humankind is "rational, and by virtue of this he is like God; he was made free in his will and master of himself."[33] Humankind was free to rule over the creation that God had

---

29. Osborn, *Irenaeus of Lyons*, 215.

30. *Haer* 5.16.2.

31. *Haer* 3.18.1.

32. *Epid.* 11.

33. *Haer* 4.4.3.

entrusted to him, and to use the reason God had given to administer creation faithfully. As I mentioned, there is a natural endowment of reason given in creation that helps the human person navigate the moral choices in this world. Irenaeus argues that humanity will be justly condemned because "though he was made rational, he lost true reason, and living irrationally he opposed God's justice, giving himself up to every worldly spirit and serving all lusts."[34]

The idea of likeness to God looks at the human person from a different perspective that is tied to the concepts of similarity and assimilation.[35] When Irenaeus uses "likeness" in the sense of similarity, he means the employment of freedom and reason given by God, which enable him to follow God's Law and keep his commandments. From the beginning, humanity needed to grow toward perfection and the likeness of God enables that growth to transpire. Since humanity is "endowed with free will from the beginning, and since God has free will—to whose likeness man was made—he is always advised to hold fast the good, which is perfected by obedience toward God."[36] But he also uses likeness in the sense of growth, through the Holy Spirit, to become more assimilated to God in obedience. I have already pointed out how his notion of growth and participation helps us understand the nature of the body and soul. Here, growth is what helps us understand the Spirit's work in leading the believer toward greater godliness. Irenaeus argues, for example, that humanity possesses the "image" of God; humankind has "the image of the handiwork but has not assumed the likeness through the Spirit."[37] Or in another place he writes, "At present we receive a certain part of his Spirit for the perfection and preparation of imperishability, so we may gradually become accustomed to

---

34. *Haer* 4.4.3. Ps. 48:21.

35. Osborn, *Irenaeus of Lyons*, 214.

36. *Haer* 4.37.4.

37. *Haer* 5.6.1.

receiving and bearing God."[38] The spiritual person is one who is being made in the image of God and being formed to be "like God" through "the communion with the Spirit," the Spirit is perfecting humanity according to the will of the Father and making humanity "according to God's image and likeness."[39] Irenaeus notes the apostle Paul calls the work of the Spirit a "pledge," so that by dwelling within humanity "this pledge already makes us spiritual."[40]

The notion of growth through God's economy helps frame the relationship between image and likeness. Adam and Eve, in Irenaeus' reading, were innocent and childlike. They were married and Eve remained a virgin, but they were not perfect, not even in the garden. Humanity is not perfect, because only the "Uncreated [God] is perfect," but humanity is created for perfection, to bear the glory of God. So in the beginning, humanity received creation, and "having been created, should receive growth; and having received growth, should be strengthened; and having been strengthened, should abound; and having abounded, should recover [from the disease of sin]; and having recovered, should be glorified; and being glorified, should see his Lord."[41]

While Adam and Eve were innocent and fitted for perfection, without the taint of sin, they were unwise and easily deceived. For Irenaeus, Adam and Eve's disobedience is emblematic of the essence of sin; disobedience is sin, and sin results in death. God has commanded them not to eat from the tree of the knowledge of good and evil, but when they took the fruit "death came upon those who ate" because they were disobedient and "disobedience to God brings death."[42] Describing the scene of the fall, Irenaeus

---

38. *Haer* 5.8.1.

39. *Haer* 5.8.1.

40. *Haer* 5.8.1.

41. *Haer* 4.38.3.

42. *Haer* 5.23.1.

writes, "when Adam had been seduced by another on the pretext of immortality, immediately he was seized with fear and hid himself—not as if he could escape from God, but, in a state of confusion at having transgressed God's command, he felt unworthy of coming into the presence of and conversing with God."[43] Satan exploited their innocence and naivety, prompting them to eat from the forbidden tree. Irenaeus sees this act of hiding as an act of contrition, as well as the fig-leaf covering as an act of humility since those leaves are so rough.[44] God drove the first couple from the garden to remove them from the tree of life, in order that they might not remain in a state of sin, but that God might provide a way of salvation for human beings to eventually live in communion with him.[45] Irenaeus believes that God is the one who calls and draws people to himself. Adam and Eve's disobedience led them into a sinful state, but God has prepared "fit dwellings" for those who have faith in God and those who do not. [46] For the "the despisers and mockers who avoid and turn themselves away from this light, and who do, as it were, blind themselves," God has "prepared darkness that is suitable to such as oppose the light."[47] But there is another existence that awaits the faithful, because "subjection to God is eternal rest."[48]

Finally, Irenaeus often speaks of humanity made according to the image and likeness of God in this future eternal state. The order and harmony of salvation history point toward the future, when humanity will, at long last, be made "according to the image and likeness of the Ingenerate God."[49] The way humanity

---

43.   *Haer* 3.23.5.

44.   *Haer* 3.23.5.

45.   *Haer* 3.23.6.

46.   *Haer* 4.39.4.

47.   *Haer* 4.39.4.

48.   *Haer* 4.39.4.

49.   *Haer* 4.38.3.

is directed toward the image and likeness of God necessitates that the "Father being well pleased and giving orders, the Son administering and fashioning, the Spirit nourishing and giving growth, while man gradually makes progress and comes to the Perfect, that is, comes to the Ingenerate."[50] He even closes his five volume work looking forward to the day when humanity will be, once again, created in the image and likeness of God.[51] Together, the terms "image" and "likeness" capture the growth and transformation of the human person, who is slowly transformed through the work of the Spirit to the image and likeness of God.

Recapitulation and Resurrection

This final section completes this overview of Irenaeus' anthropology by describing two additional theological concepts: recapitulation and resurrection. The first term captures his understanding of the atonement, but in ways that tie it closely with the whole concept of salvation. The second term helps realize Irenaeus' vision of salvation and the hope of the bodily resurrection and eternal beatitude with the Lord.

The theological concept of "recapitulation" is essential to Irenaeus' thought. The term is found in discussion of ancient rhetoric and means the "summary or recapitulation of a narrative."[52] In a rhetorical context, it was typically used to summarize a text or a speech. Behr compares it to a "resume" that summarizes the work of Christ; no part of Scripture is independent of Christ.[53] Irenaeus finds that this term is found in Scripture in such places as Ephesians 1:10, in his discussion of the relationship between Adam and Christ found in passages such as Romans 5:12-19 or 1 Corinthians 15:22, 45, as well as

---

50.   *Haer* 4.38.3.

51.   *Haer* 5.36.3.

52.   Grant, *Irenaeus of Lyons*, 50.

53.   Behr, *Identifying Christianity*, 137, 139.

in passages such as John 12 and 17. In many of these cases, the Adam-Christ typology link the ends and the beginning together in a salvific summary. The work of Christ recapitulates, or sums up, in himself the whole human race back to Adam.

In Irenaeus' thinking, it is a multivalent concept that describes a few related things: recapitulation "corrects and perfects mankind" and "inaugurates and consummates a new humanity."[54] Recapitulation means that the work of Christ corrects the error that was inflicted in Adam and perfects human nature in himself. Christ summed up, or "recapitulates in Himself all the nations that have been dispersed from Adam onward, and all the tongues, and the human race, including Adam himself."[55] When Christ became incarnate, he recapitulated in himself the long sequences of mankind and passed through all the stages of life, sanctifying them.[56] A classic summary of his doctrine of recapitulation is the well-known phrase: "[Christ] was made what we are, in order words that he might perfect us to be what he is."[57] Christ, who is the image of God, took on humanity and became what we are, in other that he might conform us to his image and, once again, fashion us in the likeness of God.

A good example of recapitulation in Scripture is supplied by Luke's genealogical account (Luke 3:23-38). Irenaeus observes that Luke wrote his genealogy backwards from the normal chronological pattern, beginning with Christ and ending with Adam. The whole account, including all the people who populate the genealogy, reflect the work of recapitulation that "joins the ends with the beginnings."[58] According to Irenaeus, Luke points out that Christ "recapitulates in Himself all the nations that had been dispersed from Adam onward, and all the

54. Osborn, *Irenaeus of Lyons*, 214.

55. *Haer* 3.22.3.

56. *Haer* 3.18.1, 2.22.4.

57. *Haer* 5.pref.

58. *Haer* 3.22.3.

tongues, and the human race, including Adam himself."[59] These generations signify that God has designed the economy with a view to the incarnation, where Christ would save humanity in his own person.

Irenaeus' understanding of anthropology is not complete without discussing resurrection and beatitude. These theological concepts are the crowning piece of his anthropology; they cast a vision of the hope of eternal life with God. Contrary to his Gnostic opponents, Irenaeus sees the resurrection as the restoration of the communion between God and God's creatures. Irenaeus writes that human bodies are "ensouled bodies, that is, they partake of the soul, which, once they have lost it, they are dead."[60] But then through the work of the Spirit they will rise and "become spiritual bodies, in order that continuing forever through the Spirit they may have life."[61] Death is not a friend to the human person; it destroys the creature God has formed. But through the work of Christ the glorious resurrection is realized when the same body "rises and receives imperishability."[62]

The Gnostics, who deny the resurrection, often appeal to 1 Corinthians 15:50, "flesh and blood cannot inherit the Kingdom of God," and they use this passage to show "that God's handiwork is not saved."[63] For the Gnostics, the body goes down to the dust and decomposes, while the soul ascends back to the heavenly realms. They cite this passage so often that Irenaeus compares their interpretation to an unskilled wrestler who tries to hold down a superior opponent with a single move. The unskilled wrestler grasps to one part of the body (or one passage—1 Corinthians 15:50), and claims victory, but everyone can see the wrestler's foolishness. Any skilled wrestler can see

---

59.   *Haer* 3.22.3.

60.   *Haer* 5.7.2.

61.   *Haer* 5.7.2.

62.   *Haer* 5.7.2.

63.   *Haer* 5.9.1.

that with a combination of moves (or a combination of other verses), the unskilled wrestler is easily bested. In Irenaeus' logic, 1 Corinthians 15:50 does not mean that flesh is rejected but that the flesh is inherited by the Spirit of God and fitted for incorruption. In other words, "this flesh by itself, that is, all alone, cannot inherit the kingdom of God; but it can be inherited in the kingdom by the Spirit."[64] He uses the illustration of a king that inherits a kingdom, and now all those who are subject to the new king are inherited by him.[65] In a similar way, flesh and blood are inherited by the Spirit, who guides the faithful toward resurrection.

Irenaeus describes the glorious resurrection in terms of incorruption and blessedness, when the faithful shall, at long last, see God. Alluding to 1 Corinthians 13:12 and 1 Peter 1:8, Irenaeus argues that, for now, we only have partial understanding, but when we are raised to new life, "our face will see the face of the Lord, and it will rejoice with an unutterable joy, namely, when it will see its joy."[66] This is the context to understand Irenaeus' well-known saying: "For living man is the glory of God, while the vision of God is the life of a man."[67] The perfect human person, seeing God and beholding the glory of God in communion with God, is Irenaeus' lasting vision.

Beholding God face to face brings together many of the topics and themes previously discussed. In the present state, those indwelt by the Spirit are being conformed to the image of Christ, so that we might be prepared by the Spirit to behold the glory of God and continually converse with God. In the present time, the faithful live in the Spirit looking forward to the future glorious resurrection when, on rising again, "we shall see him face-to-face, when all the members will overflow with a hymn

---

64. *Haer* 5.9.4.
65. *Haer* 5.9.4.
66. *Haer* 5.7.2.
67. *Haer* 4.20.7.

of joy, glorifying him who raised them from the dead and gave them the gift of eternal life."[68] A glorious and fitting conclusion when God will, in Irenaeus' words, "make us like him and will perfect us by the Father's will; for it will make man according to God's image and likeness."[69]

Conclusion

Irenaeus' concept of the human person must be situated within the storyline of redemption. While the philosophers and the Gnostics struggle to understand the relationship between the body and the soul, Irenaeus offers a compelling vision of the human person, created body and soul in the image and likeness of God, and fitted for growth in godliness. A mature and complete person enjoying the blessing of the indwelling of the Spirit, and, through the Spirit, the whole human person, created body and soul in the image of God, is conformed to the likeness of God, and preparing to see God face to face. The blessing of beatitude is enjoyed only through the recapitulating work of Christ who sums up all things in himself and who will raise up the faithful to new life in the coming kingdom of God.

But until that kingdom comes, Christians must live in the present age, striving in all faithfulness to God, who raises nations and rulers to fulfill his plan of redemption. In the next chapter, I discuss Irenaeus' political theology, which helps frame his vision of the spiritual life in the present age of the rise and fall of nations.

---

68. *Haer* 5.8.1.
69. *Haer* 5.8.1.

5

CHRISTIAN CITIZENSHIP

So far I have discussed Irenaeus' polemical context, his theological method, and his vision of the spiritual life. Now in this chapter, I want to discuss his public theology or how he viewed his life as an earthly citizen, both in the public square and among the political authorities. The call to follow Christ entailed a conversion to a different way of living—a different pattern of life. It was not a simple decision to believe in Jesus and go about your business; belief in God had significant cultural and social implications. The struggle between Christianity and Rome was more than just the struggle of a simple religion; it was a struggle for identity and conceptions of citizenship.

From the sources, we can detect a fraught relationship between Christians and the Empire. The gods were the religion of the day, and Christianity did not easily fit into their scheme. Under the Antonines, also known as the era of the Five Good Emperors—which spanned from Nerva in A.D. 96 to the death of Commodus in A.D. 192, we can see periodic examples of interactions with pagan authorities.[1] In his classic work, Edward

---

1. For further background into the interactions between Christians and pagans, see Robert M. Grant, *Augustus to Constantine: The Rise and Triumph of Christianity in the Roman World* (New York: Harper & Row, 1970). See also, Robert Louis Wilken, *The Christians as the Romans Saw Them* (New Haven: Yale University Press, 2003).

Gibbon describes this era as the Golden age of the Roman Empire. "In the second century of the Christian Era," Gibbon writes, "the empire of Rome comprehended the fairest part of the earth, and the most civilized portion of mankind."[2] With praise and adoration, Gibbon describes the peace and serenity of the empire secured under these emperors.

As the second century progressed, the Christian community was also growing slowly and the interactions with political figures and the public square were increasing. A good early example is the Governor Pliny's inquiry to Emperor Trajan around A.D. 110, requesting advice on how to deal with the Christians, who were so persuasive in their evangelism they made a noticeable impact on pagan religious practices. Pliny received an anonymous accusation containing a list of the names of Christians and interrogated several converts, trying to understand their beliefs and practices. His persecution worked to resume the frequency of pagan worship.

Other Christian leaders in the middle of the second century, such as Justin Martyr and Polycarp, had more direct interactions with political figures, which led to their martyrdom. Other early Christian apologists followed their examples, such as Melito of Sardis, Athenagoras of Athens, and Theophilus Antioch.[3] Each of them defended the faith in the public square before intellectuals and political figures, arguing that Christianity was a public good. They petitioned political figures and addressed intellectual challenges, such as those levied by the pagan philosopher Celsus in his ancient critique of Christianity, *The True Word*.

Irenaeus is heir of this apologetic tradition and while Irenaeus was focused on the Gnostic community, there is an abiding concern for his political context as well. To understand

---

2.   Edward Gibbon, *The History of the Decline and Fall of the Roman Empire* (New York: The MacMillian Company, 1914), 4:1.

3.   For more discussion of these apologists, see Robert M. Grant, *Greek Apologists of the Second Century* (Philadelphia: The Westminster Press, 1988).

his views of political authority, I begin with a discussion of Irenaeus' economic vision of creation, with God as the author and architect. Within this vision, Irenaeus imagines a formal role for earthly rule and rulers. Irenaeus recognizes that God has appointed earthly rulers with a measure of authority to accomplish some of his work. Second, I explain some of the specific ways that earthly magistrates perform God's work and are called to enact laws that curb sin and delve out blessings and curses; however, Irenaeus also recognizes the magistrate will be judged accordingly. Third, I argue that Irenaeus calls the Christian to good citizenship in the form of a virtuous life. The Christian life is the good life that will also produce the best citizens and create the pathway toward human flourishing.

Political Theology

Irenaeus' vision of political theology is grounded in a more fundamental understanding of God and creation, which emerges out of his interactions with the Gnostics. As I have shown, Irenaeus' Gnostic interlocutors do not have a positive vision of creation. The Valentinians, for example, imagine that "the origin and substance of matter from which this world was constituted," came from the "passions" of the Sophia (Wisdom), a lower aeon in the Gnostic scheme of deities.[4] These passions include grief, fear, perplexity, and ignorance.[5] All the things of creation, including the Demiurge, the degenerate god who rules in ignorance and pride, have been formed from these passions infecting the material world. Irenaeus reports that the Gnostics appeal to Paul's word in 2 Corinthians 4:4, "the god of this world has blinded the minds of unbelievers," to depict the way a wicked god rules over the creation. The Gnostics claim that "there is one God 'of this world' and another who is above every

---

4.   *Haer* 1.4.2.

5.   *Haer* 1.4.1.

dominion and principality and power."[6] But Irenaeus reads Paul to mean that one God, the creator, is the God of this world, and that unbelievers have, of their own accord, blinded themselves. Irenaeus further concludes that all things "whether angels or archangels or thrones or dominions, were established and created by God who is above all things, through His Word."[7] There is only one God, the Father, and one Christ, who "comes through every economy and recapitulates in himself all things." The Word of God is "the sovereign Ruler over supercelestial, spiritual, and invisible things, so too He might possess sovereign rule over visible and corporeal things."[8]

Given Irenaeus' perspective on creation and divine sovereignty, Irenaeus must have a positive vision of political authorities and a positive vision of the rule of the magistrate. For Irenaeus all authority flows downward from God. Through the Father's "providence all things consist, and all are administered by His command," Irenaeus writes. All things, including kings and ruling authorities are under God's command. Irenaeus will often use illustrations of earthly kings and political figures in positive ways.[9] On occasion, he uses the examples of Daniel and Joseph to illustrate the kind of leadership that thrives in a pagan world.[10] There is no hint of disparaging the simple fact that earthly authorities have been given some measure of the right to rule from their creator. Irenaeus follows the teaching of Paul and the apostles who see God's providence working through political authorities. God's providence extends not just to the mundane experience of life, but to the larger political authorities that are ruling and governing.

---

6.   *Haer* 3.7.1. Col. 1:16.

7.   *Haer* 3.8.3.

8.   *Haer* 3.16.6.

9.   *Haer* 2.2.3; 2.6.2; 3.8.1; 4.18.1; 5.9.4.

10.   *Haer* 4.5.2; 4.30.2; 5.25.3; 5.25.1–2; 5.34.2.

Irenaeus describes God's providence according to his nature. Within God's creation, and through the reign of the Word, there is nothing "unplanned or untimed," nothing that is "out of harmony with the Father."[11] God is "good and righteous and pure and spotless" and "he will not tolerate anything evil or unrighteous or abominable in his bridal chamber."[12] The bridal chamber is an allusion to the parable of the wedding feast that Irenaeus interprets in a political sense, using it to explain God's holiness and justice. I will return to the parable of the wedding feasts later, but for now what is important is the link between God's goodness, righteousness, holiness, and providence. "This is the Father of our Lord," Irenaeus continues, "through whose providence all things are in harmony, and by whose command all things are administered."[13] Because of the virtues of his nature, God will not endure anything that this is evil or unjust. Over all things, both Christian and pagan, over barbarians and Jews, over all others, God rules providentially; there is nothing hidden from his administration. Irenaeus recognizes that even the demons acknowledge God's authority. Before the coming of Christ, Irenaeus writes, "men were saved from the most wicked spirits and from all demons and from every rebel power."[14] This is not because these demons had seen God, but they knew his power by reputation. They knew of the "God who is above all things, and so at his Name they trembled, as also every creature and principality and power and every virtue that is subjected to him trembles."[15] Elsewhere he writes that "there is only one God the Builder, he who is above every Principality and Authority and Dominion and Power, he who is the Father, God, Creator, Maker, Builder, made them by himself, that is, by his Word and

---

11.   *Haer* 3.16.7.
12.   *Haer* 4.36.6.
13.   *Haer* 4.36.6.
14.   *Haer* 2.6.2.
15.   *Haer* 2.6.2.

Wisdom, namely the heavens and the earth and the sea, and all things that are in them."[16]

Irenaeus uses an analogy of the emperor's reign to explain God's rule and authority. The purpose of this illustration is to explain how Roman citizens live under the sovereignty of the emperor even though they have never seen him, nor have any awareness of his existence. Do not those who live "under the empire of the Romans, although they have never seen the emperor but are separated from him by land and by sea, know, by reason of his dominion, who it is that possesses the supreme power of ruling?" Irenaeus queries.[17] The people who live under the rule of the emperor, do not know him and have not seen him, but they "know very well" his authority, because they experience his rule. There is no hint of rejection of the emperor or his authority to rule; Irenaeus understands that he is the emperor, and his authority extends over the people even if they do not know him or recognize it. In a similar way, Irenaeus explains that the faithful ought to obey God first and then the kingdoms of this world where God reigns over all. Those who are "subject to the Name of him who made and created all things by a word," ought to recognize and submit to the true God.

Irenaeus sees an important place for the earthly life for the Christian citizen. Christians maintain a political dualism, trusting God as the ruler over all things and trusting the emperor as subservient to God. In the same way that the devil lied in the beginning, deceiving Adam and Eve, so also did he lie when he tempted the Lord by assuming that he could give him all the kingdoms of the world. It is the Lord who "institutes the kingdoms of this world, for the king's heart is in the hand of God."[18] Only by the providence of God do "kings reign and the rulers decree what is just," and under the providence of God

---

16.   *Haer* 2.30.9. See also, *Haer* 3.8.3.

17.   *Haer* 2.6.2.

18.   *Haer* 5.24.1. Matt. 4:9, Luke 6:6, and Prov. 21:1,

"princes are exalted" and "nobles govern the earth."[19] All of these passages are codified in the teaching of Paul who exhorted the faithful saying, "Let every person be subject to the governing authorities. For there is no authority except from God, and those that exist have been instituted by God."[20] The Lord himself affirms the governing authorities, Irenaeus reasons, when he ordered Peter to pay the taxes to the tax collectors for Peter and himself.[21]

Irenaeus also holds great confidence in the coming kingdom of God, so much so that he is not concerned by the trivialities of suffering in the present age. Irenaeus leans on passages from John, Daniel, and others that confirm that Christ is the stone which was cut off without hands who will destroy the temporal kingdoms and bring on the eternal kingdom, that is the resurrection of the just."[22] He cites the words of Daniel 2:44, "In those days God will set up a kingdom of heaven which shall never be destroyed."[23] Irenaeus knows that even the Roman Empire will be subject to God and destroyed when the kingdom of God comes in its fullness. He lives in the hope that guides his spiritual life.

The Role of the Magistrate

Not only does God institute governments, but God also appoints political leaders who direct the people in the ways that God desires. Irenaeus observes that human authorities, or magistrates, are "ministers of God," attending to taxing and governing of nations at the pleasure and providence of God. In Romans 13:6, for example, Paul writes, "For the same reason, you also pay taxes, for they [political leaders] are the ministers

---

19.   *Haer* 5.24.1. Prov. 8:15-16.

20.   *Haer* 5.24.1. Rom. 13:1.

21.   *Haer* 5.25.1. Matt. 17:24-27.

22.   *Haer* 5.26.2.

23.   *Haer* 5.26.2.

of God, attending to this very thing."[24] Irenaeus observes too, that the Lord affirms political leaders as the ministers of God on several occasions. For example, when Christ paid the temple tax for himself and Peter, he signaled respect for governing authorities.[25] He also points to the episode of the imperial tax— Jesus named Caesar as Caesar, identifying him as the recognized earthy authority, appointed by God to rule over the people.[26]

From the beginning, however, the devil has been active in lying to and deceiving people, trying to turn their hearts away from God. I have already mentioned the example of the devil's temptation, when he offered Jesus the kingdoms of the world. Jesus refused, in part, because ruling the kingdoms would require him to reject the earthy authorities.[27] The kingdoms of the world belong to God, who is administrating a plan of redemption, and Christ would offer his life as part of that plan. Irenaeus compares the devil to a "rebel" and a "thief" who enters a foreign region in a "hostile manner" and stirs up trouble to "usurp the king's authority."[28] While the devil rebelled against the divine law, his envy and evil have been exposed. God has given to people the "authority to tread on serpents and scorpions, and over all the power of the enemy."[29] Just as the devil had "dominion over man by rebellion, so his rebellion would be made void by man's returning to God."[30] So now, one way the serpent is tread down is through the righteous rule of the king, the administration of justice in a way that tempers immorality.

Given humanity's depravity and propensity to sin, Irenaeus argues that human authorities were instituted as "ministers of

---

24. *Haer* 5.24.1.

25. *Haer* 5.24.2. Matt. 17:24-27.

26. *Haer* 3.8.1. Matt. 22:15-22. See also, *Haer* 4.30.2.

27. *Haer* 5.24.1.

28. *Haer* 5.24.4.

29. *Haer* 5.24.4. Luke 10:19.

30. *Haer* 5.24.4.

God" for several purposes. First, magistrates impose the fear of man upon unrighteous people. Alluding to Genesis, Irenaeus argues that when humanity departed from God they engaged in "every kind of restlessness, homicide, and avarice without fear."[31] Since humankind did not fear God, God imposed "the fear of man on him," subjecting humanity to earthly kings and earthly laws.[32] So then, Irenaeus reasons, "the earthly kingdom has been established by God for the usefulness of the Gentiles," so that they might not "devour one another like fish."[33] This saying is a common ancient political reference citing the need for laws to keep society from devolving into lawless chaos.[34] God did not speak these words, Irenaeus writes, "of angelic powers or of invisible rulers, as certain ones [Gnostics] dare to explain, but of human authorities."[35] In other words, obeying political authorities is good, because they govern at the command of God. The "earthly rule," therefore, "has been established by God for the usefulness of the Gentiles," he writes. God is sovereign; he holds the world in his hands, and his creatures are called to obey him and render respect for the government authorities that God has put into place.

Second, God appoints civil magistrates to cultivate the "fear of man," so that they might enact laws that curb sin and administer justice. In Irenaeus' words, God imposed civil magistrates so that "having been subjected to human authority and educated by their law, they [humankind] might attain some justice."[36] This is why Paul writes, "he does not bear the sword in vain, for it is the servant of God, and avenger to execute his

---

31.   *Haer* 5.24.2.

32.   *Haer* 5.24.2.

33.   *Haer* 5.24.2.

34.   Wilfred Parsons, "Lest Men, Like Fishes," Traditio, vol. 3 (1945), 380–88.

35.   *Haer* 5.24.1.

36.   *Haer* 5.24.2.

wrath on the wrongdoer."[37] Irenaeus understands that God has ordained political rule for specific purposes: the magistrate is a "servant of God" and he endowed the civil magistrate with a certain measure of authority to carry out certain duties and laws.

Laws are, in Irenaeus' description, a "mantle of justice," meaning a cloak or garment of righteousness that is binding upon a people group. Civil magistrates who impose just laws that lead to righteousness are acting in a "just and legitimate manner." Laws should serve to restrain sin and hold humanity in moral restraint. The king's law, moreover, is supreme; he is not held accountable to anyone as to whether he has performed his duties "justly and lawfully," nor does he face punishment from any other authority.[38] His rule is the law of the land. God ordained political powers so that they might be "kept under restraint by their laws," in order that "they might attain to some degree of justice, and exercise mutual forbearance through dread of the sword suspended full in their view." But this does not mean that God ignores the unjust ruler. Either way—whether the king acts justly or not and whether the king knows it or not—the king will be held accountable to God, the supreme authority, for the "just judgement of God comes equally on all and is not wanting in anything."[39] The magistrate, however, who subverts justice either "iniquitously, and impiously, and illegally, and tyrannically, in these things shall they also perish."[40] The just judgment of God falls equally upon all, even those who rule over the nations.

Third, civil magistrates should work toward a vision of society where people live in "moderation toward one another."[41] Through the magistrates, Irenaeus affirms that God provides

---

37. *Haer* 5.24.2. Rom. 13:6. See also 2 Thess. 2:4 and 2:7.
38. *Haer* 5.24.2.
39. *Haer* 5.24.2.
40. *Haer* 5.24.2.
41. *Haer* 5.24.2.

blessings and judgments alike. The goal of the magistrate is to lead people toward righteousness. Irenaeus make the case that God appoints rulers who are fittingly providential for the needs of the people. In other words, in God's providence rulers arise who will guide the people toward the justice and moderation that God desires. "Kings are established by the order of the same One by whose order men are born," Irenaeus writes, "and they are suited to the ones who are ruled by them at the time."[42] Just as God is the creator over all things, so also does God administrate over kings and kingdoms, permitting some rulers at one time and others at another time, all "suited" to the ones they are ruling at the time. Some rulers, Irenaeus reasons, "are given for the correction and usefulness of the subjects and for the preservation of justice."[43] These are the good, wise, and just rulers that rule in virtue and righteousness. God gives other rulers "for fear and punishment and reproof; and some for deception, dishonor, pride, which they all deserve."[44] Through these rulers, "God's just judgement...comes equally upon all."[45] Irenaeus also sees a providential role for different civil governments to act in ways that guide humanity toward virtue. Irenaeus views citizenship through the lens of the divine life: all people within the providence of God are called to follow the path of righteousness, and God uses political authorities to help direct all people toward that end.

In Irenaeus' reading, the parable of the wedding feast offers an example of God's justice enacted through political rule.[46] In the parable, Jesus compares the kingdom of heaven to a king who gave a wedding feast for his son. His servants called all who were invited but they refused to come. After the servants were

---

42. *Haer* 5.24.3.
43. *Haer* 5.24.3.
44. *Haer* 5.24.3.
45. *Haer* 5.24.3.
46. *Haer* 4.36.5. Matt. 22:1-14.

persistent, they persecuted and killed his servants: "But when the king heard of it, he was angry, and he sent his troops and destroyed those murderers, and burned their city."[47] Irenaeus interprets this in the political sense of earthly armies that enforce justice. The apostle called the soldiers "his troops" because "all men are God's" and "there is no authority except from God, and those that exist have been instituted by God" (Rom 13:1).[48] The earth is the Lord's and so is everyone who walks upon it. The Lord "sent his troops," Irenaeus reiterates, "since everyman inasmuch as he is man, is his handiwork, even though he should be ignorant of God."[49] Summarizing his interpretation of the parable, Irenaeus writes that "being a most just Rewarder, he repays according to deserts in a very exacting manner to those who are ungrateful and who do not acknowledge his kindness."[50] These punishments are rendered, at times, by armies that dole out justice in the present age through their earthly authority, as the Lord says, "He sent His armies, and destroyed those murderers, and burned up their city."[51] The justice enacted upon those who disobeyed the invitation to come to the wedding banquet is an example of the just rule of political authorities.

There are demonic forces working to undermine God's rule and deceive people, leading them, just like Adam and Eve, toward rejection of God. But rejecting the fear of God, only leads to a great fear of man. Earthy kingdoms, Irenaeus writes, have been established by God for the benefit of people, but the devil, "who is never altogether quiet," does not want even the Gentiles to live in tranquilly."[52] The propensity of evil is to invade political

---

47.   *Haer* 4.36.5. Matt. 22:7.

48.   *Haer* 4.36.6.

49.   *Haer* 4.36.6.

50.   *Haer* 4.36.6.

51.   *Haer* 4.36.1. Matt. 22:7 (not ESV).

52.   *Haer* 5.24.2.

entities and people groups and lead them away from the worship of God, not living in a civilized way.

Christian Citizenship

Given the discussion above, Irenaeus has a positive vision of political power that falls under the direction and providence of God. Irenaeus expects that all earthly leaders are administrating and leading for the purposes God intended. Within the earthly kingdom, Irenaeus believe the church has a special calling and a unique vision of citizenship. It is a calling that often deviates from the distinctive patterns of the Roman way of life. Living on the outskirts of the Roman Empire, Irenaeus is aware of the challenges he is facing and the need to follow the way of the cross. In this section, I frame Irenaeus' concept of citizenship, explaining how he envisioned the earthly life.

First, in a way that anticipates Augustine's "two cities," Irenaeus speaks of "two ways" or "two paths" to walk in this world. This is the essence of the call of the church, to follow a separate path or a separate way of life, because all who follow God are "on pilgrimage in this world."[53] A path that is not marked by the morays or the pattens of the culture but marked by the virtues of godliness that are expressed in the Scriptures. Irenaeus often uses "road" or "way" to speak about the pilgrimage of the human person through life. On the one hand, there is a road that leads down to death. In one place Irenaeus speaks of the new path that Adam and Eve walk after they sinned and their eyes were opened, and with the opening of their eyes, "they made entrance upon the path of death."[54] But Irenaeus often characterizes the path leading to death as a multi-path road, because there are many different heretical doctrines and immoral practices. The path of sin and vice is fragmented and branching in all different directions. For those who are "blind to the Truth," Irenaeus

---

53. *Haer* 4.25.1.

54. Fragment 14.

writes, "they are constrained to go astray by different roads."[55] Their heretical doctrines and depravity led to "travel the path in varied and different and foolish manners."[56] Because they are blind, and often led by others who are blind to truth, they "fall into the ditch of ignorance," always searching for truth but never finding it.[57] Regardless of the fact that all the roads diverge in different directions, they still end up in the same place: "down to death, separating man from God."[58]

But the church walks a different path. There is one path of the spiritual life that "circumscribes the whole world," with apostolic teaching as the guide, leading the faithful in the right direction.[59] There is only one "way leading upwards for all who see, lightened with heavenly light," Irenaeus writes, and this path "leads to the kingdom of heaven, uniting man to God."[60] It does not matter where the Christian lives; in any part of the world, the path to God is the same one. In his catechetical manual, Irenaeus writes to his friend Marcianus, whom Irenaeus praises for his "zeal for godliness, which alone brings man to life eternal."[61] While he is apart from his friend, he even remarks that he wishes they were together "to help each other and to alleviate the affairs of worldly life by daily conversation about beneficial things!"[62] The journey of life is hard, especially when surrounded by those who are walking a different path.

What distinguishes the true path from the false path is virtue and, in particular, the theological virtues of faith, hope, and love. These virtues mark out the Christian citizen from the

---

55. *Haer* 5.20.1.

56. *Haer* 5.20.2.

57. *Haer* 5.20.2.

58. *Epid* 1.

59. *Haer* 5.20.1.

60. *Epid* 1.

61. *Epid* 1.

62. *Epid* 1.

pagan one. Irenaeus imagines the spiritual life as a path to walk in this world, guided by faith in God, and the theological virtues as that which keep the faithful on the straight and narrow. The things which now and always will abide "when all other things have been destroyed" are "faith, hope, and love," Irenaeus writes.[63] Irenaeus challenges his readers "to make [your] way by faith, without deviation, surely and resolutely, lest, in slacking, you remain in gross desires, or, erring, wander far from the right [path]."[64] He reiterates this point again reminding the Christian to "keep the rule of the faith unswervingly, and perform the commandments of God, believing in God and fearing Him, for He is Lord, and loving Him, for He is Father."[65] Faith is a "teacher" assuring the Christians that there is only one who is truly God. The love of God "perfects the perfect man," and the "man who loves God is perfect in this world and in the future."[66] Irenaeus is confident that true Christians will never cease to love God, because the more he is seen, the more will people love him. Finally, we must always hope "to receive something more and to learn from God that we are good and possess unlimited riches, an eternal kingdom, and infinite knowledge."[67] Through faith, Christians come to love God and hope in the coming kingdom where they will enjoy unlimited divine blessings. The knowledge of God imparts the "preeminent gift of love, which is more precious than knowledge, more glorious than prophecy, more excellent than all the rest of the charisms."[68]

One example from Scripture that illustrates the importance of virtue is the parable of the rich man and Lazarus in Luke 16. In Irenaeus' summary, the parable teaches that "no one should

---

63.   *Haer* 2.28.3.

64.   *Epid* 1.

65.   *Epid* 3.

66.   *Haer* 4.12.2.

67.   *Haer* 2.28.3.

68.   *Haer* 4.33.8.

indulge in pleasures; nor should one be a slave to his lusts and forget God by spending time in wordily entertainments and in many banquets."[69] The point of being a good citizen is not to get lost in the revelry and immorality that indulge human passions, but to live virtuously. Irenaeus calls the Christian to good citizenship in the form of a virtuous life. The human person is "endowed with reason," and freedom, but now humankind is justly condemned because "he lost the true rationality, and living irrationally, opposed the righteousness of God, giving himself over to every earthly spirit, and serving all lusts and becoming like "senseless beasts."[70]

The Gnostics, however, are the example of citizens that repel justice and live as if God does not exist. As I mentioned previously, the Gnostics reject the true God and also have a propensity to reject political rule as righteous and good. Instead, they indulge in all sorts of immorality and evil. The Gnostics declare, "they boast of having in their power and of practicing every kind of impious and godless deed."[71] They reject any earthly law and any command for righteous living, because "they claim that deeds are good or bad only because of human opinion."[72] Irenaeus is so scandalized by the immorality that he hopes that his readers "may not even think or believe that such things are done among people who live in our cities."[73] These Gnostics claim that their souls must have had 'every experience in life' so that their departure there must not be anything wanting in their experience.[74] These things, Irenaeus concludes, should not be found among fellow citizens, who are encouraging depravity and immorality among others.

---

69. *Haer* 4.2.4.

70. *Haer* 4.4.3. Ps. 49:20.

71. *Haer* 1.25.4.

72. *Haer* 1.25.4.

73. *Haer* 1.25.4.

74. *Haer* 1.25.4.

Compare these Gnostics with faithful barbarians, whom Irenaeus reports have confessed Christ and live holy lives—even without Scripture. Stressing the importance of the virtuous life, Irenaeus argues that barbarians, who do not possess the Scriptures, know how to live the Christian life through the Spirit. There are inhabitants of other nations who ultimately believe in God and live the spiritual life without ever having a written text, because, "salvation is written in their hearts by the Spirit, without paper or ink."[75] Though they lack the written documents, that is the Scriptures, they believe and are faithful as it regards "doctrine, and practices, and conduct, they are most wise and pleasing to God on account of faith."[76] Because of faith, they live in ways that please God in all "justice and chastity and wisdom."[77] He even argues that if the Gnostics were to explain to these people their doctrine and practice, the barbarians would reject them. Through their confession of faith, they live in virtuous ways that please God, and the life that please God is the most fulfilling and fruitful way to live.

Conclusion

This chapter has taken a broad view of Irenaeus' vision of political theology. He clearly has a vision of the providence of God that includes the rise and fall of kings and kingdoms. Irenaeus believes God has appointed earthly rulers with a measure of authority to accomplish some of his work. In Irenaeus' vision, magistrates perform God's work through enacting laws that curb sin and delve out blessings and curses at the discretion of the magistrate. But the magistrate will also be judged accordingly, for God's justice falls equally upon all. Christian citizenship ultimately rests in the call toward virtue, both those within the church, but also among those who are citizens of any political entity.

---

75. *Haer* 3.4.2.

76. *Haer* 3.4.2.

77. *Haer* 3.4.2.

Irenaeus calls the Christian to good citizenship in the form of a virtuous life. The Christian life is the good life that will also produce the most virtuous citizens, not those who indulge in the vices. Christian community should live in ways that demonstrate the goodness of the gospel.

In the next chapter, I bring all things together in Irenaeus' vision of cultural apologetics, a work aimed at helping guide the church toward the virtuous life lived in the world.

6

CULTURAL APOLOGETCS

In this final chapter, I bring all things together in Irenaeus' apologetic method. I describe how Irenaeus approaches cultural apologetics. The first few centuries of the church are often called the "Age of the Apologists." The theologians of the early church, such as Irenaeus, lived counter-cultural lives embedded in a pagan world. The Jews, Greco-Roman philosophers, and Gnostics all helped shape his apologetic witness. Irenaeus' theological vision, as I have explained, casts a vision of the Christian life that perceives things through a divine lens. He did not enjoy the benefits (or struggles) of living in a Christendom, but instead had to make his way by faith through the trials and tribulations of living in a pagan empire.

This chapter brings together the various threads discussed in all the previous chapters. Here I focus on Irenaeus' vision apologetics and his discussion of the "spiritual disciple," which he derives from 1 Corinthians 2:15. The spiritual disciple lives a discerning life, judging all things and being judged by no one. The spiritual disciple stands firmly on the truth of God revealed in the Scriptures and encourages those who are found in the church, those indwelt with the Spirit. The apologetic life means learning to defend the faith in fortitude and holiness and with discernment and persuasion. The spiritual disciple lives an engaging life in the public square, recognizing the theological and philosophical errors in the lives of people around them but maintaining the faith by living virtuously and persuasively. It also entails discernment and persuasion in conveying the truth, whether by word or deed, in ways that might sway them. They want to see others abandon their false views of God and come to the church, where true doctrine and practice are found.

The Spiritual Disciple

When Irenaeus casts his vision of the spiritual life, he cites the words of Paul in 1 Corinthians 2:15: "The spiritual person judges all things, but is himself to be judged by no one." The spiritual disciple lives the Christian life, navigating through the various authorities and sources embedded in any culture. The disciple is "spiritual" because the disciple has received the Spirit of God. Through the Spirit and the Scriptures, the spiritual disciple embodies the good life defined through all the virtue expressed in the Scriptures. It is an apologetic life, a life that is in every way counter-cultural and which demonstrates the way following Christ transforms one's entire way of living. The spiritual disciple knows the truth of God and can live expecting the Lord's return, knowing that the goodness of God will lead God's people toward life and righteousness.

Irenaeus reads 1 Corinthians 2:15 to mean that the one true reading of the Scriptures, the one true and authoritative conception of truth, is found in the church. Irenaeus makes this argument precisely because he is aware of all the options, all the different paths through the ancient world. The spiritual disciple judges all these other paths that deviate from the true one. The term "judges" in this case means discerning truth from error. They discern truth from error, and guide and instruct others in all truth. The spiritual disciple is the one "who receives the Spirit of God—the Spirit who was with men in all God's economies from the beginning, and announced future things and pointed out present things, and narrated past things."[1] Through the discernment of the Spirit and the truth given through the prophets and apostles throughout the economies of God, the spiritual disciple is able to discern truth from error in any other religious community. Through the Spirit and the Scriptures, the spiritual disciple can judge all other theological systems and worldviews. Irenaeus lists off Gentiles or "pagans," Jews, Marcion and his followers, the followers of Valentinus, Ebionites, docetists, false prophets, schematics, and, in summary, anyone who is "outside the Truth, namely, who are outside the Church."[2]

The spiritual person is like a tour guide who leads the faithful down the path of life, knowing where all ditches and dangers lie. Even when a new path appears, the spiritual disciple can perceive the weakness of that path and warn others not to venture down that way. What matters is that the spiritual disciple can "judge" all philosophical systems that come along. The spiritual disciple, Irenaeus explains, judges the Gentiles, who "serve the creature more than the Creator." Christians understand God as the creator of all things, and they order their lives accordingly. The spiritual disciple is aware that the Jews deny that Christ is the Messiah and reject the New Covenant. Through the Spirit, Christians believe and confess that Christ is the fulfillment of the Scripture, and they perceive the unity of Scripture in Christ.

The spiritual disciple also judges heretics, such as Marcion, and all the other Gnostic sects that refute the basic doctrine and morality of the Scriptures. These people and groups develop their vision of life from a different source, from philosophy or other religious authorities, and they are always inventing new theological systems and myths that derive from the ingenuity of their own minds. The spiritual person also judges the Jews

---

1.   *Haer* 4.33.1.

2.   *Haer* 4.33.7.

"who do not receive the message of liberty," and who reject the freedom from the law found in the grace of Jesus Christ.[3] They also do not "acknowledge Christ's coming," and "refuse to understand that all the Prophets proclaimed two comings of Christ."[4] The spiritual disciple judges anyone who gives rise to schisms and who "look to their own special advantage rather than to the unity of the Church; and who for trifling reasons, or any kind of reason which occurs to them, cut in pieces and divide the great and glorious body of Christ."[5]

The spiritual disciple does not possess all knowledge of every philosophical perspective but has a general awareness of the rule of faith; therefore, he or she is able to judge any view and explain how some of these views contradict the precepts given by God, or how they are derived from sources other than the Scriptures. The spiritual disciple can judge anyone who holds the precepts of the Lord "in contempt" and "by their deeds dishonor him who made them, and by their doctrine blaspheme him who nourished them."[6]

Above all the spiritual disciple knows the Scriptures and the teaching of the church. The disciple lives it, teaches it, and defends it, and in doing so invites others to join them on the journey toward the kingdom of heaven. For the spiritual disciple, "all things are consistent," and the spiritual disciple holds to the faith "in the one God Almighty, from whom are all things," and "in God's Son, Christ Jesus Our Lord, through whom are all things," and "by God's Spirit, who furnishes us with the knowledge of the Truth."[7] This is a complete system of doctrine; the church neither adds to nor subtracts from this doctrine. The teaching of the church that has been handed down is the "fullest account of

---

3.   *Haer* 4.33.1.

4.   *Haer* 4.33.1.

5.   *Haer* 4.33.7.

6.   *Haer* 4.33.15.

7.   *Haer* 4.33.7.

the Scripture, with neither addition nor subtraction," in other words it is "a correct and harmonious explanation according to the Scriptures, without danger and without blasphemy."[8] The knowledge of the church's faith is "the preeminent gift of love" which is more precious than anything else.[9] For the spiritual disciple, true knowledge itself consists of the teaching of the apostles that is manifested in the church and is carefully guarded and preserved.

The Apologetic Life of the Spiritual Disciple

For Irenaeus, the spiritual disciple does not run and hide from adversity or alternative views; instead, the spiritual disciple lives an apologetic life. Firm in the faith and secure in salvation, the spiritual disciple walks in faith not fear. As Irenaeus indicated previously, their vision of life is holistic, and they desire to see others join them on the pilgrim journey. Thus, the spiritual disciple lives the apologetic life in several ways, including vigilantly defending the faith, embracing the tension between fortitude and holiness, and walking the line between discernment and persuasion.

Defending the Faith

The apologetic life is a holistic life, one that recognizes that the spiritual life must embrace both beliefs and practices, and which demonstrates that only the Christian life offers the true path to human flourishing. The apologetic life requires that Christians are embedded with any and every culture and seeking to demonstrate the consistency between belief and practice. It requires defending the fundamental sources of revelation, the Scriptures, and defending the church as the bride of Christ. Take the Gnostics, for example. They use Scripture to defend their system, but they set up their "fabrication by misusing the

---

8. *Haer* 4.33.8.

9. *Haer* 4.33.8.

Scriptures."[10] They "gather together sayings and names from scattered places [in Scripture] and transfer them...from their natural meaning to an unnatural one."[11] When they conform Scripture to their systems, "They do violence to the good words [of Scripture] in adapting them to their wicked fabrications."[12] They draw from passages in the law, prophets, and the apostles, twisting and comforming them to their system. In doing so they "lead away from the Truth into captivity those who do not guard a firm faith in the one Father Almighty and in one Jesus Christ, the Son of God."[13]

As I have argued, Irenaeus recognizes that he must critique "their own system."[14] It is not that these heretics groups merely misunderstand one passage or another; instead they "fabricated their own system."[15] Their problem, as Irenaeus sees it, is a problem of perception. They do not have a true perception of God, thus they do not have a true perception of reality and, as a result, they "just cannot distinguish what is false from what is true."[16] It is imperative, Irenaeus writes, to "know the systems themselves," so that the faithful might be able to "rightly refute them" and "have counterproofs against them"[17] They create an explanation of the origin and end of all things and cast a vision for life that suits their own depraved minds. When he refutes their system, he does not aim to critique every issue, but instead aims to "overthrow their entire system by the main points."[18] These include, among other key points, their doctrine

---

10. *Haer* 1.9.1.

11. *Haer* 1.9.4.

12. *Haer* 1.3.6.

13. *Haer* 1.3.6.

14. *Haer* 1.9.2.

15. *Haer* 1.9.4.

16. *Haer* 1.pf.1.

17. *Haer* 5.pf.

18. *Haer* 2.pf.2.

of God, view of Christ, and use of the Scriptures. Given this use of sources, Irenaeus feels he must address the problems, not with this interpretation or that interpretation but with their entire systems and the assumptions that guide it.[19] He warns his readers that they should not "succumb readily to the discourse of these men, which they hear in public," because "though they speak words that sound like those of the believers, they understand not only different doctrines but even contrary ones, and such as are made up wholly of blasphemies."[20] They may have some measure of truth, bits of truth that are filtered into their system, because error "does not show its true self, lest on being stripped naked it should be detected."[21] Instead, Irenaeus continues, "it [error] craftily decks itself out in an attractive dress, and thus, by an outward false appearance, presents itself to the more ignorant, truer than Truth itself."[22] Christians must be discerning, recognizing these errors and living in ways that respond to them.

Irenaeus' main objective is to expose the truth and to bring out into the open their arguments. The "very manifestation of their doctrine is a victory against them."[23] He compares revealing false doctrines to a wild beast who was hidden in a forest. While this beast is in the forest, he attacks and kills people. But then someone comes and cuts down the forest, exposing the wild beast. So, Irenaeus writes, "people can see its attacks, guard themselves against them, throw javelins at it from all sides, wound it, and thus kill that destructive wild beast."[24] So also does Irenaeus attempt to arm his readers with a thorough knowledge of heresies, preparing the church to deal

---

19. *Haer* 2.25.1.
20. *Haer* 3.17.4.
21. *Haer* 1.pf.2.
22. *Haer* 1.pf.2.
23. *Haer* 1.31.3.
24. *Haer* 1.31.3.

with the wild beasts that are lurking, looking to kill people of faith unprepared for their attacks. He is merely attempting to "bring into the open the entire ill-formed body of this little fox," that is, the Gnostic teaching. He is so convinced by the truth of the gospel that he believes that any other worldview or system will never be ultimately satisfying.

Fortitude and Holiness

Alongside his emphasis on defending the faith, Irenaeus stresses the importance of fortitude and holiness. For the apologists, these two features must be held in unity. The nature of Irenaeus' writings themselves—his critique of all the Gnostics groups and his catechetical text that prepares the faithful to engage them— evidence fortitude. But he is not interested in fortitude at the expense of holiness.

First, the Christian must embrace the virtue of fortitude to be able to stand under trials and boldly defend the faith in whatever situation they find themselves. Citing the events in the book of Acts, Irenaeus writes that the apostles "preached with all boldness to the Jews and to the Greeks."[25] The apostles were never afraid to point out the errors in the views of people around them. But Irenaeus recognized that the apostles applied different apologetic approaches to different groups. "To the Jews," Irenaeus writes, "[the apostles proclaimed] that the Jesus who was crucified by them is the Son of God, the Judge of the living and dead, who has received an eternal kingdom in Israel from the Father."[26] The message to the Jew had a particular content and aim: to point them to Christ, proving that he is the long-awaited Messiah. With this aim, Irenaeus recognizes the need to quote the prophets and locate connections between the prophets and the person and work of Christ. The Greeks were a different matter. To the Greeks the apostles "announced one

---

25.   *Haer* 3.12.13.
26.   *Haer* 3.12.13.

God who created all things, and His Son Jesus Christ."[27] There was no use merely quoting prophecies from the Old Testament when the Greeks had a different conception of reality and first-principles. The Greeks needed to come to an understanding that there is one God who created all things and then they could move on to the work of Christ. Boldness meant speaking the right words in the right setting with all conviction.

Holiness and the holy life are the counterbalance to fortitude. The holy life should be commensurate with the teaching. There must be consistency between the words that are spoken and preached and the life that is lived. The apostles were unafraid to speak the truth, and Irenaeus followed their example. Irenaeus' primary concern is to disciple his people, teach them truth from error, and guide them toward a true love of God. The Christian must "assent to God and follow his Word, as to love him above all things, and one's neighbor as oneself—man is man's neighbor—and to abstain from all evil activity."[28] This is why God originally gave the ten commandments; the Decalogue provides a way for "friendship with himself and for concord with his neighbor."[29] But under the New Covenant, the Decalogue has been extended and strengthened: "to know God the Father and to love him with his whole heart, and to follow his Word without deviating, not only by abstaining from evil actions, but also from desiring them."[30] The freedom of living the spiritual life.

Discernment and Persuasion
Finally, defending the faith is not just a matter of fortitude and holiness, but also of discernment and persuasion. Irenaeus' aim is to provide a "concise and clear report on the doctrine

---

27. *Haer* 3.12.13.
28. *Haer* 4.13.4.
29. *Haer* 4.16.3.
30. *Haer* 4.16.5.

of these people who are at present spreading false teaching."[31] He does this so that his readers "having learned of these mysteries," can "make them clear to all your people and warn them to be on guard against this profundity of nonsense and of blasphemy against God."[32] He wants his readers to be able to identify the heretical systems, and to be prepared to prove their errors through a variety of arguments. He knows that this can be challenging because the Gnostics use words that, on the surface, sound like things they say in the church. But while they "speak the same language we do," Irenaeus writes, "they intend different meanings."[33] The Gnostics do not lure people away from the faith by conveying their whole system, but instead by arguments that sound like the sayings of the church and other authorities. Gradually, like they are capturing an animal, they lure them with little morsels of "customary food" to attract them and then bind them up and drag them wherever they please.[34] Christians must be on guard about these arguments, because it is easy even for people of faith to follow their trail.

To illustrate his point, Irenaeus uses a couple of images of a genuine substance mixed with error: "An artful imitation in glass is a mockery to a precious stone, though it is an emerald and highly prized by some people, so long as no one is at hand to evaluate it and skillfully expose the crafty counterfeit."[35] And, Irenaeus continues, "when copper is alloyed with silver, what man, if he is unskilled, will be ready to evaluate it?"[36] Anyone with knowledge of a real jewel would be able to identify a fake stone made of glass. And anyone with knowledge of silver will

---

31.   *Haer* 1.pf.2.
32.   *Haer* 1.pf.2.
33.   *Haer* 1.pf.2.
34.   *Haer* 2.14.8.
35.   *Haer* 1.pf.2.
36.   *Haer* 1.pf.2.

be able to recognize impurities. In a similar way, the Christian needs to be knowledgeable of the faith and ready to evaluate the perversions of truth they find in the culture.

Irenaeus demonstrates the apologetic life through studying his opponents and by working to craft the most persuasive arguments. Irenaeus did not avoid the challenge to understand his opponents, but took great care to study and learn their beliefs and practices. "Whoever wishes to convert them must," Irenaeus writes, "carefully know their systems."[37] He uses a physician to illustrate his point: "Surely, it is not possible for one to heal those who are ill if one is ignorant of the ailment of the one who is ill."[38] Irenaeus argues that Christians need to study the philosophical and theological diseases that plague one's culture like a physician studies the ailments of the body. *Against Heresies 1* is a good example of careful analysis of heretical views and that spiritual disciples must understand the dilemma that lays before them, and that requires a more detail understanding of Gnosticism. Irenaeus writes that the purpose of his work is so that other ministers might use his writing to help strengthen the faith of immature believers. "We shall make every effort in our power," Irenaeus writes, "to offer you many arguments as an aid against the contradiction of the heretics."[39] He aims to "strengthen the minds of the neophytes, that they may guard secure the faith that they have received from the Church well grounded, and may by no means by turned away from those who teach them badly and try to mislead them from the Truth."[40]

Discernment was only part of the apologetic equation; it was also presenting an argument with the intent to persuade others. Irenaeus understood rhetoric. He knows the importance of a good argument, and he hoped that his writing would persuade

---

37. *Haer* 4.pf.2.
38. *Haer* 4.pf.2.
39. *Haer* 5.pf.
40. *Haer* 5.pf.

people to abandon their errors and turn to the church. Irenaeus made a special point of studying his opponents thoroughly. He knew the writings and perspectives of the Gnostics. He was able to summarize their theological systems and discern the points of difference. The goal, however, was persuasion. Every interaction with a pagan world is an apologetic and evangelistic encounter. The aim of persuasion shaped his presentation. At times he would mock their system, and occasionally he would discuss the absurdity of their theological vision, but he did so with the aim to show them and others the foolishness of their thinking. Hopefully, by means of persuasive arguments, believers and others would "discard their doctrines as dung," and "follow the only secure and true Teacher, the Word of God, Jesus Christ."[41]

Knowing your opponent means understanding their strengths and weaknesses and looking for ways to persuade them. Irenaeus acknowledges that the Gnostics pose some semblance of truth, but they twist it and conform it to their myths. Writing to his friend, Irenaeus remarks that any Christian who reads the Gnostic writings will most certainly laugh, because they are so absurd. But Irenaeus knows they are "really worthy of being mourned over, who promulgate such a kind of religion," because their belief lead them away from God.[42] He prays to God that he might be able to "persuade them to give up this sort of error and desist from the blasphemy against their Maker, who alone is God and the Father of our Lord Jesus Christ," and that they might be persuaded and recognize the one true God and "shun every heretical, godless, and impious opinion." [43] He aims for these things through love. Irenaeus' apologetic life is, above all, prompted by love: "it is love that prompts us to acquaint you and all your people with the teachings which up till now have been kept secret, which, however, by the grace of God have at last

41. *Haer* 5.pf.
42. *Haer* 1.16.3.
43. *Haer* 3.25.7; 3.6.4.

come to light. For nothing is covered that will not be revealed, and nothing hidden that will not be known."[44]

Conclusion

This final chapter brings together the discussion of the previous chapters. Irenaeus' vision of cultural apologetics is framed in what he calls a "spiritual disciple" based upon Paul's discussion in 1 Corinthians 2:15. The spiritual disciple lives a discerning life and judges all things and is judged by no one. The spiritual disciple stands firmly on the truth of God revealed in the Scriptures and lives an engaging life, maintaining the faith but living virtuously and persuasively in the culture. The spiritual disciple lives an apologetic life that is marked by defending the faith, which means that Christians need to understand their culture and the patterns of belief that frame it. The apologetic life means embracing fortitude and holiness and living a holy life committed to the gospel in any and every situation. Finally, the apologetic life also means balancing discernment and persuasiveness, recognizing the theological issues in the surrounding culture, and conveying the truth in ways that might lead others toward a love for God. In all these ways, the spiritual disciple lives an apologetic life defined by the defense of the faith, a life defined by fortitude, holiness, discernment, and persuasion.

---

44. *Haer* 1.pf.2.

CONCLUSION

The first time we encounter Irenaeus in history is in the writings of the early church historian Eusebius, who records a letter from the churches of Lyons and Vienne detailing the persecution they experienced. Eusebius reports that Irenaeus carried the letter to the bishop of Rome with the inscription that Irenaeus was a presbyter in the church in Lyons and that the church there regards him "as one who is zealous for the covenant of Christ."[1] The fact that Irenaeus was selected for this task and that the church of Lyons holds him in such high regard is a testimony to Irenaeus' faithfulness. In his lifetime, Irenaeus was a fine example of a Christian leader who was committed to the gospel even in a hostile culture.

In this biography I have tried to capture Irenaeus' example of faithfulness, demonstrating his theological and biblical wisdom as well as the ways that he challenges the church to live christianly in a pagan world. Irenaeus never knew what it was like to live in a Christendom; he lived in a pagan world that was swirling with a diverse array of religious beliefs and practices. Three of these groups, Jews, philosophers, and Gnostics, were his constant dialogue partners. Each of these groups, in different ways, helps bring Irenaeus' theological perspective into relief. Jews, who rejected Christ as the Messiah, helped refine Irenaeus'

---

1. Eusebius, *The History of the Church*, 5.4.2.

Christological hermeneutic. Jews and Christians shared common texts; they both revered the writings of the prophets of the Old Testament, but they read them differently. They challenged Irenaeus to find Christ in the Scriptures like a treasure hidden in the field.

The philosophers and Gnostics offered a different challenge. They worked from reason, creating their own philosophical and religious systems that competed with the church. The pagan philosophers challenged Irenaeus to consider the relationship between faith and reason in his theological method. They also helped him see the unity of faith in contrast to the unending cycle of rational inquiry that proceeds without any unity in first principles. Irenaeus knew that there would be as many philosophical systems as there were philosophers reasoning. But in the church there is unity of faith in the apostolic teaching that guides the people of God. His main concern with the philosophers, however, was that they were often the intellectual basis for the Gnostics. Their speculations drew from the rational systems of the philosophers, but they went their own way creating all kinds of deities and myths that explained the origin and destiny of the spiritual and material worlds. In general, the Gnostics devalued the material world and assumed that only the spiritual elements embedded in certain people will be saved. The Gnostic vision of the human person led to all kinds of depravity, because they did not believe that acts performed in the body matter, the spiritual elements were their only concern. They also mingled passages from the Bible into their religious systems to give it the appearance of truth. Irenaeus reports that they were often persuasive and that some even in his own community had fallen for the Gnostic vision of life. But he hoped that, through his writing and the ministry of the church, the people of God would continue to respond to meet these challenges facing them in the culture.

Irenaeus' critique of these communities begins with first principles, or the construction of a theological system. This is the focus of the first chapter. Irenaeus argues that a theological system must get their doctrine of God right to understand any other points of doctrine. God is the source of all truth; only those who confess the one true God can understand the revelation given to God's people. Irenaeus explains his basic doctrine of God in a summary of the apostolic teaching that he calls the "rule of faith." The rule is triadic, with points dedicated to the Father, Son, and Spirit. He explains each of these persons with the words and concepts derived from Scripture; thus, the rule of faith is a summary of the doctrine of God embedded in Scripture. For Irenaeus the rule of faith and the Scriptures exist in a dialectic relationship, with the Scripture giving the rule its words and concepts. The rule is like a set of spectacles through which Irenaeus sees Scripture and the world; the rule governs his beliefs and his practices. The rule also helps order the relationship between faith and reason and helps him frame his theological method. Irenaeus argues that faith seeking understanding is the proper framework for making sense of anything in Scripture or creation.

With an understanding of his theological system in place, I turned to Irenaeus' vision for pastoral ministry. He believes the most important qualities of a pastor are sound teaching and blameless conduct. Irenaeus argues that any Christian leader who does not adhere to good doctrine and a holy life does not adhere to the teaching of the apostles, nor do they find themselves in the succession with the apostles. Already in the early church there were those who taught points of doctrine that deviated from the faith delivered from the apostles. Not every presbyter or leader is faithful, so Irenaeus must distinguish the true apostolic succession, which is only found among those who confess the faith of the apostles and live lives which were commensurate with that faith. The ministry of the church, through the leadership of the pastor, creates a community with practices such as baptism, Eucharist, prayer, and martyrdom, all of which help to frame the faithful ministry of the church. Baptism signals the entrance into the community. In baptism, the new believer makes a confession of faith and the act of baptism symbolizes the indwelling of the Spirit, the seal of adoption uniting the person to the church. The Eucharist provides the ongoing symbol of the unity of the church in the work of Christ. Irenaeus sees the Eucharist as formative for the people of God, guiding them in their life and faith and prayer. Throughout his writings Irenaeus also stresses the importance of prayer. He points to Christ as the great exemplar of prayer, who even prays for his enemies at his greatest moment of suffering. Irenaeus also models a life of prayer by frequently pausing to pray for Christ's church and for the heretics. Finally, he is familiar with those who have suffered martyrdom, and he describes their important example. They show the way of suffering and death that mimics Christ, a path that all Christians should be willing to follow. In the tumultuous days that Irenaeus faced, the pastor should embrace the high calling of leading the church.

Irenaeus also casts a vision of the spiritual life that I discussed in the fourth chapter. The human person, Irenaeus argues, is created body and soul, and it requires the indwelling of the Spirit to be fitted for perfection. While Gnostics devalued the body and the material world in general, Irenaeus elevates it. The body, just as the soul, is a work of God, and the body will be raised to new life to dwell in the kingdom of God. The concepts of the image and likeness of God help tie together Irenaeus' whole economic vision. From beginning to end the human person is formed in the image and likeness of God. Christ, of course, is essential to this economic vision. The incarnate Christ is the image of God whose life reveals the likeness of God. Through the person and work of Christ, humanity, even after the fall, retains the image of God but needs to be formed in the likeness of God. The Spirit of God, who indwells humanity, guides human creatures toward growth in godliness that perpetually prepares the faithful for resurrection. Alongside the image and likeness, the concepts of recapitulation and resurrection help fill out his vision of anthropology. The work of Christ recapitulates all things, and in him humanity enjoys salvation. Salvation is ultimately complete when the faithful are bodily raised to new life, enjoying the blessings of life with God.

In the fifth chapter, I step back to frame the general intersection between Irenaeus' doctrine of God and his vision of public life. God's economic vision includes the rise and fall of nations and rulers. Irenaeus believes God gives earthly rulers a measure of authority to accomplish some of his work. They are, to cite the words of Paul, "ministers of God." These earthly magistrates enact laws that inhibit humanity from total chaos, and they impart blessings and judgments as they see fit. Interestingly, Irenaeus does not seem all too concerned about Roman rule. He knows, following the prophecy of Daniel and other examples in Scripture, that eventually the every empire will dissolve because Christ will usher in a divine kingdom. He also knows that all earthly magistrates will be judged according to their deeds just like everyone else, but he believes that God appoints appropriate magistrates for the people they govern. God will permit magistrates who will guide them in the ways God sees fit. He calls Christians, regardless of their magistrate or their political context, to live virtuously and faithfully in the world. Christians should be the best and most virtuous citizens because they live according to a true vision of godliness.

In chapter six, I bring many of these points together into Irenaeus' perspective on cultural apologetics. The early centuries of the church were filled with apologists who lived lives of active engagement with their world. Surrounded by Jews, philosophers, Gnostics, and others, Irenaeus is a premiere example of an active apologetic life. He summarizes this life in his discussion of the "spiritual disciple," which Paul mentioned in 1 Corinthians 2:15: a spiritual disciple judges all people but is judged by no one. Firm in the rule of faith, with a cohered vision of God, creation, and the spiritual life, the spiritual disciple walks through life on a firm footing. There is nothing that other theological, religious, or philosophical systems can offer that will sway the spiritual disciple from following Christ.

With confidence, the spiritual disciple willingly defends the faith and engages their world through their arguments and actions. The spiritual disciple who lives the apologetic life learns to balance discernment and persuasion. They judge all people, discerning truth and error around them. Then they work, just like Irenaeus in his ministry, to persuade those who cling to false doctrines to confess the true God and come to the church. Persuasion might involve a whole host of rhetorical moves, both arguments and actions, but whatever the case, the love of God and neighbor should orient them.

Irenaeus' community was ravaged by suffering and persecution. The martyrs of Lyons and Vienne, which I discussed in the opening pages of this biography, capture the trying times that he and his church were facing. It is easy to fixate on the brutality of the martyrdoms, the gruesome details of the way that Christians were tortured and killed. But what stands behind that account is a community that somehow continued to live the Christian life. The vision of the apologetic life that Irenaeus gives us in his writings helps us to imagine how the church survived and even thrived in those days. I hope that many can learn from Irenaeus' example and embrace the call to live an apologetic life today.

BIBLIOGRAPHY

Barnard, L. W. *Justin Martyr: His Life and Thought.* Cambridge: Cambridge University Press, 2008.

Behr, John. *Irenaeus of Lyons: Identifying Christianity.* Oxford: Oxford University Press, 2013.

Briggman, Anthony. *God and Christ in Irenaeus.* Oxford: Oxford University Press, 2019.

Eusebius. *The History of the Church: A New Translation.* Translated by Jeremy M. Schott. (Oakland: University of California Press, 2019.

Donovan, Mary Ann. *One Right Reading?* Collegeville, MN: The Liturgical Press, 1997.

Gibbon, Edward. *The History of The Decline and Fall of the Roman Empire.* New York: The MacMillian Company, 1914.

Grant, Robert M. *Greek Apologists of the Second Century.* Philadelphia: The Westminster Press, 1988.

Grant, Robert. *Irenaeus of Lyons.* New York: Routledge, 1997.

Irenaeus. *Against the Heresies: Book 1.* Translated by Dominic J. Unger and John J. Dillion. Ancient Christian Writers 55. New York: Newman Press, 1992.

—— *Against the Heresies: Book 2.* Translated by Dominic J. Unger and John J. Dillion. Ancient Christian Writers 65. New York: Newman Press, 2012.

—— *Against the Heresies: Book 3.* Translated by Dominic J. Unger and Irenaeus M. C. Steenberg. Ancient Christian Writers 64. New York: Newman Press, 2012.

—— *Against the Heresies: Books 4 and 5*. Translated by Dominic J. Unger and Scott D. Moringiello. Ancient Christian Writers 72. New York: Newman, Press 2024.

—— *Fragments*, "Fragments from the lost writings of Irenaeus," Alexander Roberts and James Donaldson, eds, *The Ante-Nicene Fathers, vol. 1, The Apostolic Fathers, Justin Martyr, Irenaeus* (Edinburgh: Christian Literature Publishing Company, 1885; reprint, New York: Scribners, 1899).

—— *On the Apostolic Preaching*. Translated by John Behr. Popular Patristics Series 17. Crestwood, NY: St Vladimir's Seminary Press, 1997.

Kelly, J.N.D. *Early Christian Doctrines*. Revised fifth edition. London: A&C Black, 1977; reprint Continuum, 2006.

Markschies, Christoph. Gnosis: *An Introduction*. New York: T&T Clark, 2003.

Osborn, Eric. *Irenaeus of Lyons*. Cambridge: Cambridge University Press, 2001.

Parsons, Wilfred. "Lest men, Like Fishes." *Traditio*. Volume 3. 1945.

Robert M. Grant. *Augustus to Constantine: The Rise and Triumph of Christianity in the Roman World*. New York: Harper & Row, 1970.

Schoedel, W. R. "Theological Method in Irenaeus (*Adversus Haereses* 2.25-28)." *The Journal of Theological* . Volume 35, no. 1. 1984.

Slusser, Michael. "How Much Did Irenaeus Learn from Justin?" *Studia Patristica* 40. 2006.

Tatian. *Oratio ad Graecos and Fragments*. Edited by Molly Whittaker. Oxford: Clarendon Press, 1982.

Wilken, Robert Louis. *The Christians as the Romans Saw Them*. New Haven: Yale University Press, 2003.

ALSO AVAILABLE IN

THE *EARLY CHURCH FATHERS* SERIES...

EARLY CHURCH FATHERS
SERIES EDITORS
MICHAEL A. G. HAYKIN & SHAWN J. WILHITE

CYRIL
OF HIS LIFE & IMPACT
ALEXAN-
DRIA

DANIEL HAMES

CYRIL OF ALEXANDRIA

Daniel Hames

Cyril of Alexandria (c. 376-444 AD) was a towering figure in early Christianity, renowned for his theological prowess and leadership as the Patriarch of Alexandria. Born into a prominent Christian family, Cyril received a comprehensive education in theology and philosophy, which equipped him for his future role as a defender of orthodox Christian doctrine.

Daniel Hames (PhD Vrije Universiteit, Amsterdam) is Vice President and Lecturer in Theology at Union School of Theology. He is author, with Michael Reeves, of *God Shines Forth: How the Nature of God Shapes and Drives the Mission of the Church*'.

EARLY CHURCH FATHERS
SERIES EDITOR MICHAEL A. G. HAYKIN

BASIL
OF
HIS LIFE
& IMPACT
CAESAREA

MARVIN JONES

BASIL OF CAESAREA

Marvin Jones

Basil of Caesarea (A.D. 329–379) was a Greek Bishop in what is now Turkey. A thoughtful theologian, he was instrumental in the formation of the Nicene Creed. He fought a growing heresy, Arianism, that had found converts, including those in high positions of state. In the face of such a threat he showed courage, wisdom and complete confidence in God that we would do well to emulate today.

Marvin Jones is Chair of the Christian Studies Department and Assistant Professor of Church History and Theology at Louisiana College in Pineville, Louisiana. He holds degrees from Southeastern Baptist Theological Seminary, Dallas Theological Seminary and the University of South Africa.

EARLY CHURCH FATHERS
SERIES EDITORS
MICHAEL A. G. HAYKIN & SHAWN WILIHITE

ATHANASIUS
OF HIS LIFE & IMPACT
ALEXANDRIA

PETER BARNES

ATHANASIUS OF ALEXANDRIA

Peter Barnes

From the foreword: Until his death in 373, Athanasius was the most formidable opponent of Arianism in the Roman Empire. Ultimately, for him, this fight was not a struggle for ecclesial power or even for the rightness of his theological position. It was a battle for the souls of men and women. Athanasius rightly knew that upon one's view of Christ hung one's eternal destiny. As he wrote to the bishops of Egypt in 356: "as therefore the struggle that is now set before us concerns all that we are, either to reject or to keep the faith, let us be zealous and resolve to guard what we have received, bearing in mind the confession that was written down at Nicaea." And by God's grace, his victory in that struggle has been of enormous blessing to the church ever since.

Peter Barnes serves as the minister of Revesby Presbyterian Church, Revesby, New South Wales, Australia and also lectures in Church History at Christ College, Sydney.

AUGUSTINE

OF HIPPO

HIS LIFE
& IMPACT

BRADLEY G. GREEN

AUGUSTINE OF HIPPO

Bradley G. Green

Arguably the most significant theologian in Church history, Augustine is nonetheless a figure of dispute in protestant circles, distrusted for his views on ecclesiology, amongst other subjects. Yet his love for the Lord and articulation of the doctrine of grace ensure that his writings remain relevant and inspiring to many Christians today.

For anyone looking to begin to understand this theological giant, Bradley Green's biography offers a clear insight into Augustine's life and beliefs. In the words of the patristic himself, 'Take and Read'.

Bradley G. Green teaches theology at Union University in Jackson, Tennessee. Brad and Dianne also helped co-found Augustine School, a Christian liberal arts school in Jackson, Tennessee.

Christian Focus Publications

Our mission statement
Staying Faithful

In dependence upon God we seek to impact the world through literature
faithful to His infallible Word, the Bible. Our aim is to ensure that the
Lord Jesus Christ is presented as the only hope to obtain forgiveness of
sin, live a useful life and look forward to heaven with Him.

Our Books are published in four imprints:

◁OX CHRISTIAN FOCUS

Popular works including biographies, commentaries, basic doctrine and
Christian living.

◁OX MENTOR

Books written at a level suitable for Bible College and seminary students,
pastors, and other serious readers. The imprint includes commentaries,
doctrinal studies, examination of current issues and church history.

◁OX CHRISTIAN HERITAGE

Books representing some of the best material from the rich heritage
of the church.

◁OX CF4KIDS

Children's books for quality Bible teaching and for all age groups:
Sunday school curriculum, puzzle and activity books; personal and
family devotional titles, biographies and inspirational stories –
because you are never too young to know Jesus!

Christian Focus Publications Ltd,
Geanies House, Fearn, Ross-shire,
IV20 1TW, Scotland, United Kingdom.
www.christianfocus.com